ESCAPE FROM

THE

SELF

a study in contemporary American

poetry and poetics

Escape from the Self

the
Self ;

a study in contemporary American

poetry and poetics

KARL MALKOFF

new york

columbia university press

1977

Columbia University Press
New York   Guildford, Surrey
Copyright © 1977 Columbia University Press.   All rights reserved
Printed in the United States of America

Library of Congress Cataloging in Publication Data

Malkoff, Karl.
Escape from the self.

Includes bibliographical references and index.
1. American poetry—20th century—History and criticism.
2. Poetics. I. Title.
PS323.5.M35   811'.5'09   77-22880
ISBN 0-231-03720-1

for Barbara

Contents

Preface

IT is by now a commonplace
that in proportion to its distance in time from our own age earlier historical periods seem increasingly simpler, while the
present generally reveals itself in its overwhelming complexity.
But while it is taken for granted that the simplicity is illusion,
less attention is given to the corollary, that the complexity is
probably illusion too. Contemporary American poetry, for example, seems to consist of poetic sensibilities so diverse no common ground is conceivable. In a superficial sense, this is perfectly true, with the consequence that there has probably never
before been so much confusion as to what specific poets are trying to do, let alone how successful they are in doing it.

However, one is always suspicious of such feelings of
uniqueness. The obvious approach was to examine the work of
non-poets that had captured our cultural imagination, and then
plunge into the apparent complexity to see if a good part of the
poetry participated in any of the several collective visions of reality dominant in our time. It was almost immediately clear that
the common ground was the challenge to the integrity of the
self, and therefore to its ability to organize experience. Less obvious was the fact that the altered status of the self was not
universally perceived in a negative fashion, that it could be apprehended as an escape as well as a loss. And finally, it was possible to conclude—with a full sense of the caution that ought to
accompany all such generalizations—that while American fiction was by and large involved with the sense of loss, American

poetry had increasingly made itself the vehicle of escape, and that poets as different as Charles Olson and Robert Lowell were united on at least this point. Just as poetry itself, according to a definition that will figure prominently in this work, may be thought of as the perception of harmony in the face of apparent divisiveness, so it seemed possible to see contemporary American poetry as the expression, at least in part, of a shared sense of man's capacity to experience himself and the world.

However, although it is worthwhile enough to take cognizance of this shared vision, this book has a more important purpose. Much of the criticism of this contemporary period has been based on a conception of the self totally inappropriate to the poetry to which it is applied. To be sure, as I shall point out, our critical sensibility is changing as well; but it lags behind the poetry, and has not yet been applied systematically to poetry that has abandoned the self as the inevitable perspective from which reality must be viewed and organized. Ezra Pound's *Cantos,* to anticipate a major example, has consistently been approached in such a way as to make its rejection unfair, its approval unconvincing. It is my intention in this book to demonstrate the irrelevance of critical approaches based on an earlier sense of the self to a poem like, say, the *Cantos,* and to suggest what perspectives might prove appropriate.

I should add that this study is not in the least intended to be polemical, or even to evaluate the poetic tendencies I describe and analyze. Understanding must precede evaluation, and it is precisely because I felt our understanding of the work in question needed to be re-assessed that this book exists. Nonetheless, I hope I have shown no lack of the sympathy for my subject without which criticism must be necessarily superficial.

I have, of course, acknowledged in the text all the sources I knowingly used. But there is always that debt, so difficult to cite specifically, to writers who have preceded me in the study of contemporary American poetry and poetics. I thank my colleagues at City College, many of whom listened to a portion of this book, and presented their valuable advice; I especially thank Ed Quinn, who contributed some information I needed, when I needed it. And finally, I am grateful to Barbara Comen and Bob Triana, who have been crucial to the writing of this book.

New York
December 1976

Acknowledgments

☙

GRATEFUL acknowledgment is made to the following for permission to quote copyrighted material:

To Atheneum Publishers, Inc. for selections from *Reasons for Moving* by Mark Strand, copyright © 1968.

To Doubleday and Company, Inc., for selections from *The Collected Poems of Theodore Roethke* by Theodore Roethke, copyright © 1960 by the Administratrix of the Estate of Theodore Roethke.

To Faber and Faber, Ltd.: for selections from *The Collected Poems of Theodore Roethke* by Theodore Roethke; for selections from *Life Studies* and *Notebook 1967–68* by Robert Lowell; for selections from 77 *Dream Songs* and *His Toy, His Dream, His Rest* by John Berryman; for selections from *The Complete Poems* by Randall Jarrell; for selections from *Ariel* by Sylvia Plath, copyright © 1965 by Ted Hughes; for selections from *Personae* and *The Cantos* by Ezra Pound.

To Farrar, Straus & Giroux, Inc.: for selections from *Life Studies* (copyright © 1956, 1959 by Robert Lowell) and *Notebook 1967–68* (copyright © 1967, 1968, 1969 by Robert Lowell) by Robert Lowell; for selections from 77 *Dream Songs* (copyright © 1959, 1962, 1963, 1964 by John Berryman) and *His Toy, His Dream, His Rest* (copyright © 1964, 1965, 1966, 1967, 1968 by John Berryman) by John Berryman; for selections from *The Complete Poems* by Randall Jarrell, copyright ©

1945, 1951, 1955 by Randall Jarrell, copyright renewed © 1973 by Mary von Schrader Jarrell.

To Harper & Row, Inc., for selections from *Ariel* by Sylvia Plath, copyright © 1963 by Ted Hughes.

To New Directions Publishing Corp.: for selections from *Personae* (copyright © 1926 by Ezra Pound) and *The Cantos* (copyright © 1934, 1937, 1940 by Ezra Pound) by Ezra Pound; for selections from *Selected Poems: Summer Knowledge* by Delmore Schwartz, copyright © 1938 by New Directions Publishing Corporation, © 1966 by Delmore Schwartz; for selections from *Collected Earlier Poems* by William Carlos Williams, copyright © 1938 by New Directions Publishing Corporation.

To W. W. Norton & Company, Inc., for selections from *Collected Poems* (copyright © 1972 by A. R. Ammons) and *Sphere* (copyright © 1974 by A. R. Ammons) by A. R. Ammons.

To the Estate of Charles Olson and Corinth Books for selections from *The Maximus Poems* by Charles Olson, copyright © 1960 by Charles Olson; the Estate, Viking Press, Inc., and Cape Goliard Press, for selections from *Maximus Poems IV, V, VI* by Charles Olson, copyright © 1968 by Charles Olson.

To Random House, Inc., for selections from *Selected Poems* (copyright © 1953 by Karl Shapiro) and *The Bourgeois Poet* (copyright © 1964 by Karl Shapiro) by Karl Shapiro.

To Wesleyan University Press and Robert Bly for selections from *Silence in the Snowy Fields* by Robert Bly, copyright © 1962.

ESCAPE FROM

THE

SELF

a study in contemporary American

poetry and poetics

CHAPTER ONE

Hard Times for the Imperial Self

MAN is part of the natural world. But he alone, we presume, is aware of his existence as a distinct part of that world. He is self-conscious. He knows that he has a body, that he is his body, but he is capable of a peculiar detachment; he can dualistically perceive crucial boundaries between consciousness and the object of consciousness. He now knows that he possesses an unconscious, a repository of thoughts and feelings not immediately available to his conscious mind, but he generally experiences his unconscious as an outside force acting upon him rather than part of himself. He can reason, but even here he usually distinguishes between the rational process and the part of him that is aware of that process.

For most of man's history, he has identified his consciousness with the spiritual. The notion of the soul as a discrete human component can be traced to the beginnings of recorded mythology or folklore. But the absolute separation of spirit and matter, which was probably given its most effective formulation by Descartes, has been especially significant in western intellectual traditions. Eastern thought, particularly religious thought, while aware of this separation, has viewed it as largely illusory. There is an underlying oneness of being that transcends the superficial separateness of bodies and conscious minds. The Self is the One. In the west, there have been many mystics who would subscribe to that doctrine. But Paul Tillich, concerned with the anguish of the individual confronting his separation from nature, expresses the western bias very well in describing the limits of mysticism: it does not affirm *finite* being.[1] For the mystic, the particular consciousness can consider itself part of unified being. But it is clear that western man has decided to stand or fall by the success of the finite, separate individual to organize experience and give shape to the universe in both its material and spiritual aspects.

This has always been a difficult enterprise, though at some times it has seemed easier than at others. Never has it seemed more difficult than now. The ultimate failure of the conscious self adequately to deal with the experience it perceives, a pervasive if not exclusive characteristic of twentieth-century thought, has been so well documented it is scarcely necessary to recount it here.[2] Phenomenology, defining reality as a relation between observer and observed, placing the emphasis on the phenomenon itself rather than the source or recorder of that phenomenon, undermined not only the notion of an objectively knowable universe but of a coherent and consistent perceiving self as well. Existentialism, an immediate descendent of phenomenology, envisions a meaningless universe to which the individual can give form only by the assertion of his unsupported self, an arbitrary act whose validity cannot be demonstrated. The fact that even atheistic existentialism is, as Jean-Paul Sartre insists, optimistic in its faith in the power and value of that absurd leap does not in the least diminish the *Angst* of the individual confronted by the void, forced to play the role of God, but without any certainty as to who he himself is.

But it is important to realize that the loss of a potent self, which has often been characterized as *the* contemporary illness, does not necessarily lead to terror and despair. Some of our most influential thinkers have not only welcomed this loss of self, they have advocated it with an urgency that derives from their conviction that many of the horrors of the modern world spring

1. *The Courage to Be* (New Haven: Yale University Press, 1952), p. 160.
2. See, for example, Wylie Sypher, *Loss of the Self in Modern Literature and Art* (New York: Random House, 1962).

precisely from the traditional definition of the self. For them, it is probably more accurate to describe the phenomenon under consideration not as the *loss* of the self, but the *escape* from the self.

This revolution of consciousness has had its effect on the arts; in some cases it has been anticipated by the arts. In fact, the chief thesis of this book is that the defining characteristic of contemporary American poetry is its abandonment of the ego—the conscious self—as the inevitable perspective from which reality must be viewed. However, before exploring the extent to which contemporary poetry and poetic theory are manifestations of a new understanding of what constitutes the self, it would be useful to explore some of the important attempts to articulate that understanding. To this end, I have decided to emphasize the work of Norman O. Brown and Marshall McLuhan because the attention they have received and the notoriety they have provoked make them likely sources for an examination of our age's cultural imagination. I will be concerned with their ideas not with regard to their objective truth, but as manifestations of a vision of reality which by its very existence becomes part of our experience. They are examples in my argument, not the bases on which it rests, sources of metaphor, not scientific proof.

In *Life Against Death,* Norman Brown argues against the inevitability of the traditional self, here the Freudian ego, as the only instrument available to man for the ordering of his experience. Man's consciousness of his existence has led to a sense of dissonance in which the rest of nature does not participate. "Man is distinguished from animals by having separated, ultimately into a state of mutual conflict, aspects of life (instincts) which in animals exist in some condition of undifferentiated harmony or unity."[3] The immense burden placed upon the ego is the reconciliation of these conflicting instincts, or, in the terms Freud finally adopted, of life against death.

Brown makes it clear that the conflict between Eros and

3. *Life Against Death* (New York: Random House, 1959), p. 83. Page references will hereafter be given parenthetically in the text.

Thanatos is simply another way of describing the conflict between man's sense of harmony with nature and his sense of
separation.

> Freud's theorem that Eros or the life instinct, as it operates in the
> human libido and in the lowest cells, aims to preserve and enrich
> life by seeking unification implicitly contains the theorem that the
> aim of the death instinct is separation. . . . The principle of unifica-
> tion or interdependence sustains the immortal life of the species and
> the mortal life of the individual; the principle of separation or in-
> dependence gives the individual his individuality and ensures his
> death. (p. 105)

The consequence of this conflict is a paradox. Death bequeaths
to man his individuality. But man cannot easily come to terms
with death. It is, in fact, the business of the ego to repress
awareness of that aspect of the human condition. Therefore,
Brown argues inexorably, man represses his true individuality,
his true identity.

The ego deals with death, and with the anxieties produced by
man's awareness of death. In order to do this, it organizes, it
specifies, it limits man's sense of himself in time and space. It is
involved, for example, in the bodily phenomenon of sexual organization. To begin with, the newborn child—man in his natural
state—is polymorphously perverse: "Children . . . explore in in-
discriminate and anarchistic fashion all the erotic potentialities"
(p. 27). As the child grows up, his erotic impulses are progres-
sively concentrated in specific parts of the body. Thus Freud's
descriptions of oral, anal, and genital erotic organizations. These
stages are all means of mediating the dualities that result from
man's awareness of himself as separate from the rest of nature:
the oral stage deals with the dualism of subject and object, the
anal stage with the active and the passive, and the genital stage
with masculinity and femininity (pp. 116–17). For Freud, the
normally developed human being enters adulthood with his sexuality genitally organized; "perversions" are a result of the failure completely to attain that stage. But even in Freudian terms,
genital organization is unnatural tyranny, a repression of the
natural state of polymorphous perversity (which an inhibited so-

ciety can give its due in sexual foreplay, and not formally label it perverse unless it does not lead to genital intercourse).

Freud, says Brown, understands this paradox as a necessary conflict, which he explained early in his career as between the pleasure-principle and the reality-principle, later as between Eros and Thanatos. Man is then doomed to neurosis, or at best sublimation. For without some form of repression, some form of compromise with reality—in this case the compromise of the wish for endless bodily delight with the need for reproduction—civilization could not exist. Brown, however, is not so certain of the inevitability of this compromise. Citing William Blake, who said, "Energy is the only life, and is from the Body. . . . Energy is Eternal Delight," Brown at least hints—later he will be more direct—at the possibility that man is not inexorably bound to dualism. "Neurotic symptoms, with their fixation on perversions and obscenities, demonstrate the refusal of the unconscious essence of our being to acquiesce in the dualism of the flesh and spirit, higher and lower" (pp. 31–32).

Analagous to the imposition upon the body's natural polymorphous perversity of specific sexual organizations is the imposition of the sense of time upon the participation of human consciousness in pure being, in the eternal present. Instead of experiencing unending nowness, we locate ourselves at some specific point along a continuing line.

Historical time had traditionally been thought of as a given aspect of the human condition, as an absolute reality independent of any subjective state. However, as Brown points out, "recent developments in physics, biology, and anthropology are tending to establish the relativity of time-schemata to variable biological and cultural needs. In other words, the twentieth century has seen the disintegration of the universality and, with the universality, the rationality also, of the time-schema" (p. 95). Brown understands this sense of historical time as the ego's attempt to hold on to the past in the face of death. "The study of the repetition-compulsion suggests that repression generates historical time by generating an instinct-determined fixation to the repressed past, and thus setting in motion a forward moving dialectic which is at the same time an attempt to recover the past" (p. 103).

In childhood, there is no conflict between the repetition-compulsion and the pleasure-principle. However, when repression exists, the repetition-compulsion becomes attached to the past in such a way as to distance the neurotic from the present and condemn him to search for the past in the future. Consequently, the child's impulse totally to participate in his being is limited and thwarted. But again, Brown does not accept the inevitability of this limitation. "If . . . we go beyond Freud, and speculate on the possibility of a consciousness not based on repression but conscious of what it is now unconscious, then it follows a priori that such a consciousness would be not in time but in eternity" (p. 94). Or, to put it another way, "the restless quest for novelty would be reabsorbed into the desire for pleasurable repetition; the desire to Become would be reabsorbed into the desire to Be" (p. 93).

Brown, then, provides a psychoanalytic explanation for man's dualistic interpretation of his experience. Dualism has its origins in man's awareness of his separation from nature and leads to the split between spirit and matter. This analysis is not in itself revolutionary; it is, after all, derived largely from Freud's own work. But in suggesting that this separation need not take place, Brown seems to be in the company of mystics rather than scientists. And even mystics generally resolve the dualistic split by denying the ultimate reality of the material world, by denying the existence of the subject as a discrete entity. More important, the mystical experience itself remains a special case, by definition distinct from ordinary human consciousness. Apocalyptic in the sense that Blake is apocalyptic, Brown moves toward nothing less than a new description of human consciousness.

But there is a formidable obstacle in Brown's path. According to the body of psychoanalytic thought upon which Brown bases his own arguments, the dualistic apprehension of reality seems to be a necessary condition for the creation of a culture, of a sophisticated civilization. In Freudian terms there are essentially two methods of dealing with what Freud understood to be inevitable instinctual conflicts: repression and sublimation. Repression leads to neurosis, while sublimation leads to civilization. However, as Brown points out, the relationship between repression and sublimation is ambiguous. Both are means of dealing with sexual instincts, and both operate by changing the aims and objects of those instincts. The clearest distinction between the two mechanisms seems to be not psychological but social. Brown quotes Róheim: "The difference between a neurosis and a sublimation is evidently in the social aspect of the phenomenon. A neurosis isolates; a sublimation unites" (p. 143). Even if the distinction were theoretically clear-cut, Freud himself was skeptical both as to the capacity of the mass of human beings to sublimate a significant portion of instinctual conflict, and as to the possibility of sublimation ever being totally free of neurosis.

As the problem is defined by Freud, it seems indeed insoluble. Civilization, as well as the individuals in it, must be neurotic; man is, therefore, the diseased animal. However, Brown sees an alternative. Where Freud envisioned "an alliance between the ego and the reality-principle against the id," and thus the inevitability of repression, Brown proposes "to ally the ego and the id against reality" (p. 153). The project, then, is not to adjust to reality but to alter it, not to find socially validated channels for repressed energies but to make conscious much of what is now repressed. In fact, it is precisely as a science of culture rather than as individual therapy that Brown finds the real usefulness of psychoanalysis. For culture can be understood as the projection of infantile complexes into concrete reality. And Brown reasons that "Human consciousness can be liberated from the paternal (Oedipal) complex only by being liberated from its cultural derivatives, the paternalistic state and the patriarchal God. Thus culture does for all mankind what the transference phenomena were supposed to do for the individual" (p. 155).

Whether or not what Brown calls the "Dionysian" consciousness could ever be realized, it is a powerful formulation of an ideal relationship between man and the universe. As we have seen, it would be conscious of much that is now unconscious. Allied with the id rather than with reality, it would exist in eternity rather than time, and would reject formal logic and the law of contradiction as rules under which the repressed human mind consents to operate. And by refusing to repress the body, the Dionysian consciousness would escape the duality of spirit and matter.

In *Love's Body*, Brown elaborates the possibilities suggested in *Life Against Death*. Since he defines all dualistic thinking as a consequence of repression, Brown can say "The boundary line between self and the external world bears no relation to reality; the distinction between ego and world is made by spitting out part of the inside, and swallowing in part of the outside."[4] In other words, what is experienced externally as separation is equivalent to what is experienced inwardly as repression. The solution, of course, is to break down the boundaries.

> To give up boundaries is to give up the reality-principle. The reality-principle, the light by which psychoanalysis has set its course, is a false boundary drawn between inside and outside; subject and object; real and imaginary; physical and mental. It gives us the divided world, the split or schizoid world—the "two principles of mental functioning"—in which psychoanalysis is stuck. (*Love's Body*, pp. 149–50)

Brown calls on modern science to support his attack on common-sense reality. For surely our common sense insists that each human being exists as a separate entity. But the respected philosopher of science Alfred North Whitehead characterizes such separation as the assumption of relatively naive scientific systems and denies the possibility, in the light of modern physics, of speaking of the isolated location in time and space of any object.

> The reality-principle says, if *here,* then not *there;* if inside, then not outside. . . . Whitehead says the reality is unification: reality is events (not things), which are prehensive unifications; gathering diversities together in a unity; not simply *here,* or *there,* but a gath-

4. *Love's Body* (New York: Random House, 1968), p. 143.

ering of here and there (subject and object) into a unity. (*Love's Body*, pp. 154–55)

And lest the reader suspect that Brown is distorting Whitehead for his own purposes, it is useful to realize that Whitehead goes so far as to say that "In a certain sense, everything is everywhere at all times,"[5] a proposition that may contain some comfort for the reader of *Finnegans Wake* or *The Cantos*.

Brown's own commitment to literature leads him to speculate on the function of art in the light of his new conception of man's relation to his universe. Inconsistently, perhaps, but not surprisingly, he views art not as simply another neurotic symptom, but rather as one of the few possible means of releasing the repression that produces neurosis. Modern poetry, or rather the entire Romantic movement, in which Brown seems to include modern literature, has the job of de-emphasizing the abstract in favor of the concrete, the analytic in favor of the holistic. Language may be disease, but the sensual speech of poetry heals. And while dreams and neurosis do, in fact, express repressed materials, art liberates them. "Perhaps we should say that neurosis and dreams are the determinate outcome of the unconscious, while art is its conscious articulation."[6]

Here, however, at the very moment he proclaims the triumph of art, we may become aware of some of the limitations of Brown's sense of poetic possibilities. Art, for Brown, is not only a function of consciousness, it is the function of a strong consciousness. While Brown's poetics would give increased importance to unconscious materials, those materials clearly require mediation, some sort of control that would render them consciously articulate. Even taking into account a new definition of consciousness, a Dionysian consciousness, dualism is implicit in Brown's conception of art. We might speculate that if a Dionysian consciousness were ever achieved, art would become both unnecessary and impossible. Nonetheless, until the coming of

5. *Science and the Modern World* (New York: New American Library, 1948), p. 93.
6. *Life Against Death*, p. 11.

that new consciousness, art would be one of the most effective tools man possesses in attempting to anticipate, and even in bringing into existence, that consciousness. "As for poetry, are not those basic poetic devices emphasized by recent criticism—paradox, ambiguity, irony, tension—devices whereby the poetic imagination subverts the 'reasonableness' of language, the chains it imposes?"[7]

As these last lines make obvious, the poetry Brown has in mind is the poetry of Modernism, the criticism the New Criticism. The devices he cites are those created by the rational mind in an attempt to use rationality to undermine rationality. However, Modernistic poetry has been succeeded by poetry with far more varied formal possibilities, poetry with which the New Criticism has not been able to come to terms. And, as this book will attempt to demonstrate, rationally based devices have given way to the use of new perspectives, new stances. So that we must bypass Brown's comments on poetry, and return to his definitions of consciousness, if we wish to understand the impact of that sense of consciousness on the arts.

If historical time is not inherent in reality, but rather an imposition on it, then temporal sequence is not a necessary means of organizing a narrative. If, as from the point of view of eternity, all time is copresent, then the poet can juxtapose any events without any concern but the effect of the juxtaposition. The very notion of plot, which is after all a preoccupation with cause and effect relationships, is suspect when deprived of its sequential underpinnings. Similarly, spatial organization, the sexual organization of the body, becomes the prototype for the imposition of logical categories upon experience. In place of abstraction is the concrete; in place of temporal and logical organizations is the simple act of juxtaposition, which, as we shall see, opens up new worlds. For meaning must now be understood not as the idea about the thing, nor even, strictly speaking, as the thing itself, but rather as residing in the gaps created by apparently arbitrary juxtapositions. "Meaning is not in things but

7. Ibid., p. 319.

in between; in the iridescence, the interplay; in the intercon-
nections; at the intersections, at the crossroads."[8]

In addition, if traditional means of ordering external experience are no longer beyond question, neither are conventional
categories of inner experience. Instead of personality, we have
persona; the self is an illusion, a role, a piece of primitive magic
(*Love's Body,* pp. 90, 108). Boundaries between the self and the
outer world, boundaries between the self and the inner world,
have no final validation. And without boundaries there can be
no self in the ordinary sense of the word. In fact, in a breath-
taking reversal with which R. D. Laing would feel quite comfortable, Brown suggests that it is not schizophrenics who are
split, but rather the so-called "normals" who perceive nonexis-
tent boundaries. "Schizophrenics are suffering from the truth"
(*Love's Body,* p. 159).

As I have already indicated, our interest in Brown in this book
is not as a scientist but rather as an imaginative writer. And the
student of contemporary American poetry has probably already
recognized that Brown's imaginative vision has much in common with the vision projected by contemporary verse. The viola-
tions of temporal sequence, the lack of logical frameworks, the
stark juxtaposition of fragments, the failure to create a consistent, unifying personality of Pound's *Cantos,* on the one hand,
and the breakdown of barriers between inner and outer experiences, the acceptance of the schizophrenic as a legitimate mediator of experience of much Confessional verse, are all justified
by Brown's vision. What is most interesting about these areas of
agreement is the fact that as a literary critic Brown remains immersed in Modernism. We may then hypothesize that the new
consciousness of *Life Against Death* and *Love's Body* was not
invented to explain the new literature, but rather emerges from
the same formative influences.

As confirmation of the fact that these formative influences do,
in fact, exist, we may point to the recent prominence accorded
to many thinkers who attack the idea of the traditional western

8. *Love's Body,* p. 247.

self for many of the same reasons as Norman O. Brown. When he, for example, argues that genital tyranny is the same as political tyranny, or rather creates the frame of mind that makes possible political tyranny, Brown finds himself in the same camp as Franz Fanon, who considers colonialism the inevitable consequence of the psychological make-up of the western mind.[9] When he attacks the excessive importance given to a rational ordering of reality, Brown anticipates such physiologically oriented psychologists as Robert Orenstein, who finds it likely "that each person has two major modes of consciousness available, one linear and rational, one arational and intuitive," and that in the west the former has been developed and emphasized at the expense of the latter.[10] And when he suggests that modern man—modern western man—has violently and unnecessarily split himself from the natural world of which he should be a harmonious part, Brown becomes the ally of biologist René Dubos, who warns that we may cut ourselves off from our environment only at the peril of our very survival.[11] But the most well-known of Brown's fellow critics of the conventional definition of human consciousness is Marshall McLuhan. And since, while Brown reaches his conclusions by examining man's inner life, McLuhan is chiefly concerned with the ways in which man perceives outer experience, McLuhan's work presents an opportunity to give greater depth to our understanding of this conception of human consciousness, which seems central to much of contemporary American poetry.

In *Love's Body,* Brown points out the link between his own work and that of McLuhan. Citing McLuhan's observation that the garden, the symbol of man's harmonious relation with the rest of creation, is destroyed by excessive emphasis on the visual, Brown writes: "The garden is polymorphism of the senses, polymorphous perversity, active interplay; and the opposite of

9. See, for example, *The Wretched of the Earth* (New York: Grove Press, 1968), or *Black Skin, White Masks* (New York: Grove Press, 1967).

10. See *The Psychology of Consciousness* (San Francisco: W. H. Freeman, 1972).

11. See especially *So Human an Animal* (New York: Scribners, 1968).

polymorphous perversity is the abstraction of the visual, obtained by putting to sleep the rest of the life of the body" (p. 121). Where Brown talks of repression and repetition-compulsion, McLuhan asserts that "With the instressed concern with one sense only, the mechanical principle of abstraction and repetition emerges into explicit form."[12] And while Brown and McLuhan might very well disagree about whether visual dominance is simply the means by which the rest of the body is repressed in the interest of a small part of the mind, or whether the repression is simply an inevitable consequence of the ways man has learned to perceive his world, what is most striking is the extent to which their descriptions of the reality beyond the illusion coincide.

Brown, for example, emphasizes the sexual organization of the body as the primary spatial distortion. McLuhan, most interested in human perception, points out that our understanding of the space surrounding us is arbitrarily organized. Citing Gyorgy Kepes and E. H. Gombrich, he says that the " 'fixed point of view' depends on the isolation of the visual factor in experience," and that "Far from being a normal mode of human vision, three-dimensional perspective is a conventionally acquired mode of seeing, as much acquired as is the means of recognizing the letters of the alphabet, or of following chronological narrative" (pp. 156, 25).

As the last phrase suggests, what is true of space must also be true of time. The capacity to isolate oneself at a particular moment, which capacity McLuhan attributes to literacy in general and movable type in particular, is prerequisite to a sense of chronology, of historical time (pp. 288–907). And if sequence and spatial categories are suspect, then logic as well must be seen as a special—not normal—mode of organizing reality. When McLuhan suggests that "Schizophrenia may be a necessary consequence of literacy" (p. 32), he gives added dimension to Brown's assertion that "schizophrenics are suffering from the truth." In sum, "The visual makes for the explicit, the uniform,

12. *The Gutenberg Galaxy* (New York: New American Library, 1969), p. 27.

and the sequential in painting, in poetry, in logic, history. The non-literate modes are implicit, simultaneous, and discontinuous, whether in the primitive past or the electronic present . . ." (p. 73).

We may note that while McLuhan's explanations of why we are so alienated from our experience often seem superficial and arbitrary when compared to the closely reasoned analysis of Brown's *Life Against Death*, he does provide us with a possible solution to a question that Brown does not even seriously raise: why is it that at precisely this moment in our history we have become aware of the limitations of traditional definitions of the self and its relation to the rest of creation? According to McLuhan, electronic media such as radio, telephone, cinema, and television have challenged the dominance of the visual bred by print, helped restore a more harmonious balance among the senses, and consequently made possible a new awareness of man's place in nature. Whether or not we are totally satisfied with this explanation, which in one deft stroke presumes to account for the last one hundred years or so, it nonetheless serves to point out that whatever the cause and effect relationships— and about the validity of those relationships McLuhan is at least implicitly inconsistent—the worlds in which physical theory was shaped by Albert Einstein, Werner Heisenberg, Neils Bohr, and Max Planck, in which psychological theory developed from Sigmund Freud to Ludwig Binzwanger, R. D. Laing, and Norman O. Brown, in which colonialism metamorphosed from the moral obligation of civilization to its shame, must necessarily coincide. They are all part of the dominant vision of man and his place in the universe of contemporary Western culture. Not surprisingly, aesthetic theory in general and poetic theory in particular has been affected by this dominant vision. But most of it remains stalled, like Brown, in Modernist literature, and is unequipped to deal with post-Modernist work, or in some cases work contemporary to Modernism, that carries the new vision close to its logical formal conclusions. One of the exceptions, however, is *The Seamless Web,* by Stanley Burnshaw, which at the least lays the groundwork for the next step.

The primary thesis of *The Seamless Web* is that poetry is the expression of underlying harmony in the face of apparent divisiveness.

> For the poem as a whole and in its units is, above all, an act of uniting. And to respond by experiencing its act of uniting is to relive, for the duration and with the whole of one's being, an indefinable sense of organic creature unity such as pervaded our creature-existence when it "knew" itself part of the seamless web of creation. That a man is alien, that divisiveness burdens his nights and days, that his organism is instinct with the drive toward primary unity, make his need for re-living acts of this kind more crucial than he can know. For isolate man, as he lives ever more in himself, from others, and apart from the world that contains him, creature-knowledge has become no less necessary for his survival.[13]

Burnshaw's frame of reference is by now familiar. Divisiveness would be explained by Brown as the repression of the body, by McLuhan as the dominance of the visual; unity, for Brown, lies in polymorphous perversity, for McLuhan in the harmonious balance of the senses. The poem, in Burnshaw's scheme of things, as in Brown's, is the means of linking two worlds: the world of repression with the world of bodily knowledge. Whereas philosophy, or prose in general, is the attempt of the conscious, rational mind to encompass experience, poetry is the expression of the total organism.

Burnshaw, in fact, devotes a significant portion of his book to demonstrating that much of creativity is beyond conscious control (pp. 10–46 and passim). In particular, what is frequently referred to as the "content" of the poem is a function of consciousness, while such devices as rhythm, rhyme, sound effects, all things that may be apprehended subliminally in the reading of the poem, are functions of body. Burnshaw, then, provides the aesthetic to complement the theories of Brown and McLuhan. The divided self, the fixed point of view, the sense of temporal reality are all given their due—but only when brought into relation with that part of man that participates in the oneness of the universe, that exists in eternity.

13. *The Seamless Web* (New York: Braziller, 1970), p. 193.

However, it is important to realize that what Burnshaw is proposing is, quite reasonably enough, a general theory of aesthetics, a theory that will explain all the art ever created, or, at the least, all the poetry ever written, to which broad applicability any theory of aesthetics based on universals must aspire. And Burnshaw is, in fact, chiefly concerned with the poetry of such as Shakespeare, Donne, Keats, and Yeats, with the great traditional poets of English literature. This in spite of the fact that he has provided a perfectly rational, even scientific basis for a great deal of specifically modern poetry: poetry in open form. The rhythms of free verse, for example, can be explained in Burnshaw's terms as manifestations of bodily rhythms, of breath, heartbeat, even alpha waves, that subtly influence the voice, and therefore the line, of the poet. But if Burnshaw, who refers to Pound six times, Wiliams once, and Olson not at all, does not realize that he has provided scholarly foundations for that most unacademic school of poetry, Projective Verse, it is because he is not interested in pursuing an obvious corollary to his propositions: that if poetry is indeed a perception of the underlying harmony of things in the face of apparent divisiveness, then the relationship between harmony and divisiveness must vary, just as, for example, in Yeats's *Vision* the proportions of subjectivity and objectivity, lunar and solar components, must vary, and that at certain points in human history one or the other of these modes will be dominant. One can conceive of a continuum: at one end of the line is total harmony, at the other end total divisiveness; at neither extreme could poetry exist, since poetry is a relation between the two. In the eighteenth century, perhaps, dominated by the intellect, poetry would approach the divisive end of the line. The Romantic reaction would have moved verse a considerable distance back toward harmony. However, in all cases, the divisive, implicit in the speaking voice of the coherent self, would have great significance. By challenging the integrity of that voice, and the coherence of the self it expressed, contemporary American poetry appears to have approached, and therefore tested, the extent to which poetry can exist free of the organizing principles imposed by conscious intellect. It is a poetry of sensation rather than abstraction, of fragmentary perceptions rather than neatly formulated wholes. And since poetry must, if it is to reach a significant audience, be apprehended for the most part visually, and since, even if the poem is heard, its characteristics must be filtered through consciousness before the total organism of the reader can respond to it, it may well be that some of the poetry has gone beyond the point where it can successfully communicate and entered that no-man's land where poetry can no longer exist. But there is no good way to understand limits without going beyond them.

The thesis which has been restated by this discussion, and which remains to be demonstrated by this book, is that however great the apparent diversity of poetry being written in America today, from, for example, the turning inward of Confessional poetry to the turning outward of Projective verse, most of the poetry shares one common characteristic with the rest: the abandonment of the conscious self, the traditional ego, as the inevitable perspective from which reality must be viewed. But we are now in a position to say precisely what we might have initially vaguely suspected, that this escape from the self is the expression of a broader act of cultural imagination, of the recognition as being outmoded and nearly useless the definitions of self conventionally employed in psychology, philosophy, politics, history, in fact, all the disciplines from which we expect guidance about how to conduct our lives. The fact that we are still very much in the midst of this process of redefinition means that this study must itself make use of multiple perspective, and draw on the poetry for some understanding of the self, as well as on the philosophers of self for understanding of the poetry.

CHAPTER TWO

Diverse Points
of View

BEFORE moving on to the chief
concern of this book, a consideration of the poetry itself, it will
be useful to make explicit some of the assumptions upon which
my argument must be based. I refer in particular to the assumption that poetic form is not simply, as Charles Olson quotes Robert Creeley, "an extension of content," but rather is in itself the
most important "content" the poem has to offer. Just as the
defining characteristics of a philosophy lie not in the answers it
provides but in its formulation of questions, so in choosing the
form his poem will take the poet makes his most important
statement about the nature of reality, to which the ideas of his
poems can at best bring but feeble reinforcement.

Now this is for the critic an attractive premise, but one that
must be stated with care. It is easy enough to refer to the ex-
pansiveness of Renaissance verse, the assertion of harmony in
eighteenth-century rhymed couplets, the apparently spontane-
ous shapelessness of much modern poetry, and there would un-
doubtedly be some truth in those references. The three qua-
trains and couplet of the Shakespearean sonnet, for example, do
seem to force the poet's mind into definite logical patterns. But
to read into that fact alone a total vision of reality is risky. And
when it comes to attributing specific meanings to such formal
values as iambs or trochees, which many critics have indeed
tried to do, the critical effort becomes pointless, since even if

meaning can be attributed to a particular metrical effect, the result is so clearly dependent upon contextual variables as to be useless in other cases. The danger in trying to read too much into purely formal qualities lies precisely in the fact that what form expresses is very often necessarily what is not expressable in straightforward language.

But to be aware of the difficulties in building an intelligible case on purely formal values is not totally to abandon the method. It is still possible to remark, as I shall, that the choice of a meter represents the imposition of a preconceived, rationally comprehensible pattern on language, while the choice of free verse is a result of faith in the possibility of intuitively grasping the appropriate rhythm of a line, faith, one might say, in the ability of the total organism, rather than simply the conscious part of that organism, to determine form. And surely the very notion that a poem can be planned as it proceeds, which was the case in such poems as *The Cantos* and *The Maximus Poems*, describes a different universe from the one in which John Milton so carefully planned *Paradise Lost*.

However, while these and similar observations can be made, there is a particular formal quality that is relatively amenable to analysis and is at the same time clearly connected to the thesis of this study: the point of view from which the poem was written.

Although point of view in poetry has attracted little attention (with the significant exception of Erich Auerbach's brilliant *Mimesis*, which is limited to narrative literature, and which does not deal with modern poetry), point of view in the novel has become part of the standard repertory of the literary critic.[1]

In the eighteenth and nineteenth centuries, the dominant point of view was that of the omniscient narrator. We may state the assumption behind this point of view as being that if there were a god he would know every thing there is to know about human experience and would be able to express that knowl-

[1]. For the standard analysis of point of view in fiction, see Percy Lubbock, *The Craft of Fiction* (London, 1929). Auerbach's book is *Mimesis: The Representation of Reality in Western Literature* (New York: Doubleday, 1957).

edge; the novelist, then, is the god of the universe of the novel. But even this assumption has assumptions contained within it. It assumes a material world that exists independently of any observer of that world, and actions that could be abstracted from the actors. It assumes characters whose motives could be located, who would be, in Aristotle's terms either consistently consistent or consistently inconsistent; but they would in any case be capable of being isolated from other characters, from the world at large, and even from actions they themselves had committed. That is to say, in the case of characters, that the character precedes the action, and the action can be said to be caused by the character, rather than the alternative, that the character is, in fact, the sum total of his actions, and may be said to be created by those actions.

The omniscient narrator may make his presence felt by commenting on the events and characters he is describing, but almost always it is the events and characters themselves, and not the narrator, that command our attention. There is rarely any question as to who or what the novel is about. Again, it is the discrete and clear existence of persons and actions that makes likely this arrangement; the novelist is simply, if somewhat disingenuously, the medium through which his creations in their wholeness may be presented to the reader.

To this point, I have been speaking of the omniscient narrator who proceeds to relate his story in the third-person. And although this is in fact the case in most eighteenth- and nineteenth-century fiction, there are numerous exceptions, first-person narratives in the form of letters, journals, or even unspecified means. However, in most cases the first-person narrator is simply a device, a convenience, and is simply a limited version of the omniscient narrator, lacking certain information, at least for a time, but possessing nonetheless total faith in the solidity of the world.

A good example of this is the early epistolary novel *Pamela,* by Samuel Richardson. This well-known story of the poor but virtuous maid who successfully resists both seduction and straightforward force to maintain her honor and emerge ultimately as the lawful wife of her erstwhile persecutor, is told by the heroine herself, in letters to her family. While Pamela is naive, and, especially at the start of the novel, lacks a good deal of information about the way her world operates, we may always trust her descriptions of events that have taken place, of her own actions and motivations, and, finally, those of the people around her. It does not occur to us to question what constitutes an event, or how it is possible to know that event. And we must accept totally the accuracy of the heroine's self-knowledge, and the honesty with which she communicates that knowledge.

Of course, it was possible, in spite of the conventions, to question anything one pleased. And I have chosen *Pamela* as my example precisely because there exists, in Henry Fielding's *Shamela,* concrete evidence of such questioning. Unable to tolerate what he considered the unspoken hypocrisy of Richardson's self-righteous heroine, Fielding created a woman whose life is similar to Pamela's, but who is quite consciously manipulating her master until she gets what she wants. So one could very well question the veracity of a particular narrative. But let us examine the limitations of that questioning.

First, it is chiefly Pamela's honesty that is in doubt, not her capacity to judge what is taking place. Second, it is not Richardson's Pamela that is under attack, but Richardson himself. And this is the main point. There is no real distinction to be made between point of view of author and character, except in the relatively minor matter of extent of knowledge. It would not occur to the serious reader, for example, to ask whether or not Richardson's attitude toward his heroine was ironic; without the notion of subjectivity in the modern sense, such a question would be meaningless.

As late as the nineteenth century, in a work such as *Bleak House,* the situation was essentially unchanged. Esther Summerson is certainly a naive narrator; but nonetheless, we have no reason to doubt the reasonable accuracy of her perceptions of experience. And in Dickens' world most of all, not only do events take on definite shape, characters are as solid as they are at any point in English literature.

Of course, there are exceptions. The tensions between illusion and reality in *Don Quixote* should not be ignored. Laurence Sterne seems an exception to almost any rule. But even the exceptions serve to remind us that the questioning of interpretations of experience and of motivations have not really reached modern extremes. The tangible world is always there, giving respectability to the most intense probings.

It is difficult to say precisely when the change takes place. It is usually placed in the last decade of the nineteenth century, but the division is not clear cut. For example, in *The Brothers Karamazov*, Dostoevsky, rarely thought of as an experimenter in formal matters, distances himself from the novel's narrator, who, although he does not figure significantly in the action, is a fellow townsman of the Karamazov family. The distance is admittedly small, but just enough to enable Dostoevsky to shroud in darkness certain knowledge of the murderer of old man Karamazov. Is it because he wishes to divert our attention from the legal to the moral and theological? Or has it occurred to Dostoevsky that it is not, in the situation described in the novel, possible to talk about cause and effect in simplistic terms, to isolate a specific agent of an event from an interrelated web of experience? If it is the former, Dostoevsky is doing no more than any novelist of his time, or perhaps since the onset of the novel, had already done. If the latter, however, he is one of the first consciously to encounter the epistemological and moral problems more customarily associated with the twentieth century.

At any rate, by the time we reach the work of Henry James and Joseph Conrad in the last decade of the nineteenth century, there is no doubt as to the important role point of view plays in the novel. No longer a question of expedience, of a mere narrative device, it involves now the very meaning of the novel. It is in *What Maisie Knew* (1897) that James first makes explicit the narrative device that was to dominate the remainder of his career. As the author pointed out in his preface, the virtuosity of the novel lies in the presentation of reality through the limited field of perceptions of a young girl. In this center of consciousness technique, James retains the third person voice, so that he may describe those perceptions in his own language. But he can reveal nothing that is not known to the chosen center of consciousness, in this case Maisie. For the first time in a clear and explicit way, the narrative device has become not a convenience but an integral part of the meaning of the novel. For in *What Maisie Knew* the epistemological and the moral have become inextricably entwined. And never again in James work will these two concerns be very far apart.

The supreme example of this kind of art is, of course, *The Ambassadors* (1903). Lambert Strether goes to Paris as an emissary of Puritanical Woollett in general, and the matriarchal Mrs. Newsome in particular. His task is to discover what is keeping Mrs. Newsome's son, Chad, in Europe. The assumption is that he has an illicit relationship with a woman; from Woollett's point of view, nothing else will explain the facts. By the time he reaches Paris, however, Strether is open enough to believe there is no woman. But a visit to Chad's tastefully decorated apartment suggests that there must be a woman after all—no one from Woollett could be accused of that kind of good taste—and that her influence is benign. When Strether meets Mme de Vionnet and her daughter, he assumes, approvingly, that it is the young girl. Then he realizes that the woman is indeed Mme de Vionnet, but that the relationship is a virtuous one. Finally, when he sees the couple in the country, out for the afternoon without warmer attire for the ride back to Paris, he realizes, with a typically Jamesian deduction, that they are spending the night together and have been doing precisely that all along.

It would seem, then, that Woollett was right all along. And in a sense it was. But Strether has undergone profound changes and has abandoned the absolute and rigid morality of Woollett in favor of a more flexible morality grounded in specific human relationships. And because Strether has changed, the nature of the "event" he is observing, that is, the relationship between Chad and Mme de Vionnet, has changed too. Reality, James asserts, is a relationship between an observer and a thing observed; neither can be said to have meaningful existence without the other. And he asserts this by means of form, by technique, as least as much as by substance.

At about the same time that James was discovering the virtues of the center of consciousness, Joseph Conrad was working out the kinks in his favorite first-person narrator, Marlow. In "Heart of Darkness" (1902) Conrad had complete control of his methods. The emphasis here is not on the reliability of the narrator as an interpreter of experience; we do not question Marlow in the same way that we question Maisie, Strether, or the narrator of James's *The Sacred Fount* (1901), who leaves us far from convinced of his sanity at the novel's conclusion. It is rather a question of the reader's growing awareness that experience is necessarily particular, that we can speak only of the reality of the individual apprehending reality. At first, we may think the story is about Kurtz; Marlow seems only the vehicle by means of which the plot can be unfolded. But with the help of Marlow's Eastern meditative postures, which sandwich the narrative, we finally recognize that the story has been "about" Marlow all along. It is his inner journey, his moral education. Subjectivity is not only a legitimate mode of grasping reality, it is in some cases the only appropriate mode.

From this point on, the die is cast. It becomes difficult to write a first-person narrative, or limit the perceptions of a third-person narrative, without realizing the profound implications of those strategies. We should perhaps note the *tour de force* of this method, the distorting narrator of Ford Madox Ford's *The Good Soldier* (1915), who so thoroughly violates the principles of objectivity that he almost obliterates distinctions between truth and falsehood. In Mark Schorer's words:

> The fracture between the character of the event as we feel it to be and the character of the narrator as he reports the event to us is the essential irony, yet it is not in any way a simple one; for the narrator's view, as we soon discover, is not so much the wrong one as merely *a* view, although a special one. No simple inversion of statement can yield up the truth, for the truth is the maze, and, as we learn from what is perhaps the major theme of the book, appearances have their reality.[2]

2. "An Interpretation," in Ford Madox Ford, *The Good Soldier* (New York: Random House, 1957), p. vii.

Schorer might have added that in this world appearances are the only reality.

Obviously, there is a connection between the increasingly sophisticated use of point of view in the novel and man's broader understanding of his place in the universe. James and Conrad anticipate Einstein's theory of relativity, which asserts that all measurements in time and space exist only in relation to a fixed point in time and space, and Werner Heisenberg's indeterminacy principle, which states that in certain circumstances the instrument of observation not only distorts the observation but actually makes it impossible. As in the novel, subjectivity becomes a legitimate basis of scientific thought.

Understandably, the first applications of this attack on the solid universe are on outer experience, on perceptions. But soon after, the further implications of these theories become apparent. If the fact that reality is a relationship between observer and things observed affects our interpretation of objects and events outside of us, that is, the things observed, surely it must affect our interpretation of the life within, the observer. Are we accurate to speak of such a thing as a particular personality, or is what we call personality an arbitrary constancy imposed upon a fluid reality? We begin, in fact, to approach that questioning of the nature of the self with which this study began. But there is an intermediate step between the subjectivity of a James novel and the radical conception of self proposed by Charles Olson, in which, as we shall see, the Jamesian ego plays so small a part.

If personality, or self, is an arbitrary constancy, we may think of it as a role, a mask, that the artist may take on in the interests of exploring his world. The novelist had, in a sense, always been in the business of creating masks to the extent that he created characters and gave them dramatic presence in his story. However, until the time of James, Conrad, and Ford, the mask in the novel could have no more special significance than the narrator's voice; that is, it was not perceived as a medium through which reality could be distorted. With the new uses of subjectivity to be worked out, it is perfectly understandable that the implications of the mask remained to be explored by poets.

Beyond that, it may simply be true that the novel is an ideal medium for the exploration of a world of objects and events newly experienced as fluid and resonant rather than fixed and clearly defined, while the poem, with its inevitable emphasis on the speaking voice of the poet, more logically becomes preoccupied with the presentation of self. In any case, we must now shift our attention to point of view in the poem.

In *Mimesis*, Erich Auerbach convincingly traces the perception of actions by the poet through the continuous immersion in the present of Homer, the paratactic constructions of medieval literature, to the finally fluid and sequential arrangement of events of Dante. Auerbach's remarks on the *Odyssey* require our special attention, since we will soon be in the position of arguing that much of modern poetry bears closer resemblance—at least with regard to point of view—to the *Odyssey* than to poetry written from the time of Dante through the nineteenth century.

Auerbach analyzes the passage in which Odysseus' old nurse, Euryclea, recognizes her master's scar. Between the moment of recognition, and the reaction to that knowledge on the part of the nurse, Homer inserts a detailed account of how the scar was produced. Our instinctive explanation would probably attribute this interruption to Homer's wish to generate suspense. But Auerbach argues that this cannot be the case.

> . . . An episode that will increase suspense by retarding the action must be so constructed that it will not fill the present entirely, will not put the crisis, whose resolution is being awaited, entirely out of the reader's mind, and thereby destroy the mood of suspense; the crisis and the suspense must continue, must remain vibrant in the background. But Homer . . . knows no background. What he narrates is for the time being the only present, and fills both the stage and the reader's mind completely.[3]

Here, we recognize the absence of the fixed point of view necessary to the establishment of perspective in time or space. The growth of this perspective, and the consequent awareness of layers of experience to be arranged by the ordering intellect, is

3. *Mimesis*, pp. 2–3.

traced by Auerbach, through Dante, as I have said, until the twentieth century and Virginia Woolf. However, like Brown, Auerbach stops with Modernism, and does not explore alternative movements that seem to turn the Western tradition around on itself in ways that Auerbach did not anticipate. This will become clearer after we have had the opportunity to examine methods of organizing experience employed by Pound and the Projectivist poets. For the time being, we can say that the conventional sense of time with which reality is endowed by the traditional self is a learned sense, which can be unlearned, and that we can deduce this fact from an examination of literature as well as through psychoanalytical theory or an analysis of media.

Auerbach is interested in the ways the self orders experience. He is less directly concerned with the nature and composition of that self, that is, with its integrity, its boundaries. Of course, the notion that it is not the poet himself but some outer agency— generally conceived of as a divine agency—that accounts for the mystery of creation goes back to the origins of critical thought, for example, the concept of divine madness in Plato's *Phaedrus,* and has never been very far from the surface. The most recent equivalent of this idea, which we touched upon in the preceding chapter, is Stanley Burnshaw's assertion that the poem is an expression of the entire organism, that many poetic devices have other than rational or conscious origins. And yet, this has been a theoretical rather than practical question; whatever the source of inspiration, it is the poet himself who must give communicable form to the vision of reality. (Even Burnshaw, as I have already indicated, does not examine in detail poetry that gives the appearance of the poet having relinquished conscious control.) There has been some question of whether the poet's voice was public or private, and the Romantic movement did open for the poet's investigations areas of experience that had previously not seemed suitable for poetry. But through the continuing shifts in the ways poet's organize experience, through the debates concerning the sources of poetic inspiration, through the movement of the poet's voice from spokesman of a

people to man preoccupied with himself, back and forth—
through all this what is most impressive is the fact that there
has been no serious questioning of whose voice relates the
poem, or of the poet's right consciously to mediate experience.
Especially in lyric poetry, it has seemed self-evident that the
voice of the poem was the poet's own.

And yet, there are instances in which that is not true. In
drama, for example, the poet creates voices, attitudes, in short,
centers of consciousness, that are not his own. There is no incongruity here, because the drama, which must be made to
move harmoniously by the controlling imagination of its creator,
nonetheless does not pretend to be anything but the con-
vergence of diverse points of view. As long as the distinction between dramatic and lyric voice is maintained there is no confusion, no radical commentary on the nature of reality. But in the
nineteenth century precisely that confusion begins to take
place.

Curiously, the attack on traditional self beings not with partial
insights or blind questionings, but rather with what remains
one of the most sophisticated formulations of the problem. In
his letter to Richard Woodhouse (October 27, 1818), John Keats
wrote:

> As to the poetical Character itself (I mean that sort of which, if I am
> any thing, I am a Member; that sort distinguished from the
> Wordsworthian or egotistical sublime; which is a thing per se and
> stands alone) it is not itself—it has no self—it is everything and
> nothing—It has no character—it enjoys light and shade; it lives in
> gusto, be it foul or fair, high or low, rich or poor, mean or elevated—
> It has as much delight in conceiving an Iago as an Imogen. What
> shocks the virtuous philosopher, delights the chameleon Poet. It
> does no harm from its relish of the dark side of things any more
> than from its taste for the bright one; because they both end in
> speculation. A Poet is the most unpoetical of anything in existence;
> because he has no Identity—he is continually informing and filling
> some other Body. . . .[4]

It has been necessary to quote the entire passage in order to see
clearly the ways in which Keats's escape from self is not exactly

4. *English Romantic Poetry and Prose*, ed. Russell Noyes (New York: Oxford
University Press, 1956), p. 1,221.

the same as the one that constitutes the subject of this study. Most important, he sees this "selflessness" as almost an affliction suffered by a certain kind of poet; it is not a truth about the human condition to which the poet is simply more sensitive. Second, there is in Keats's letter a strong sense of the poet as dramatist, as a writer who must give life to persons and objects about whose separate existence there can be no serious question. Even the example given is taken from drama. Finally, the letter is in many ways an apologia: do not blame me if you do not approve of my subjects—I am, after all, only a poet, an emptiness filled by the real world.

However, after we have said this, we must still be impressed by the extent to which Keats seems to anticipate a more modern idea of the poet's self. If he writes of the poet as dramatist, it is, after all, the lyric poet, Keats himself, to whom these observations are applied. It is not distorting Keats's meaning to say that for him the lyric voice is dramatic; it involves the donning of a mask. And it is not distorting Keats to say that what he perceives at the core of the self—which perception makes necessary the wearing of the mask—is nothing.

Although it must be placed in the context of the more general Romantic concern with the distinction between subjective and objective poetry,[5] Keats's insight does not produce immediate or direct changes in the theory or practice of poetry. But the changes do take place. Robert Browning, whose essay on Shelley reveals his own concern with the question of subjective or objective poetry,[6] helps to draw the distinction with his own work. Does the poet draw simply on his self—the Wordsworthian sublime—or does he imaginatively enter into outer experience? Browning's real contribution to the theory of objective poetry is the series of dramatic monologues that remain today his most frequently read work. It is, of course, not the first time anyone has written dramatic monologues. But Browning has first detached the monologue from its usual dra-

5. See M. H. Abrams, *The Mirror and the Lamp: Romantic Theory and the Critical Tradition* (New York: Norton, 1958), pp. 241–44.
6. H. F. B. Brett-Smith, *Peacock's Four Ages of Poetry, Shelley's Defense of Poetry, Browning's Essay on Shelley* (Oxford: Oxford University Press, 1945).

matic context, blurring further the distinction between lyric and dramatic. And the sheer quantity of this sort of poetry produced by Browning removes it from the realm of the *tour de force* and suggests that the mask may be the dominant means of expression of the poet.

An interesting commentary on the impact of what seems to us now a perfectly ordinary poetic mode is provided by Wimsatt and Brooks in their treatment of Browning's essay on Shelley. They quote the Shakespearean F. J. Furnivall, who delights in the fact that

> . . . Browning's "utterances" here are *his,* and not those of any one of the "so many imaginary persons" behind whom he insists on so often hiding himself, and whose necks I, for one, should continually like to wring, whose bodies I would fain kick out of the way, in order to get face to face with the poet himself, and hear his own voice speaking his own thoughts, man to man, soul to soul.[7]

Furnivall's wish "to get face to face with the poet himself, and hear his own voice speaking his own thoughts," expresses in its clearest form the bias concerning the poet's self the refutation of which has been, if not the goal, at least the effect, of much of contemporary poetry. The image that appears near the end of Ibsen's *Peer Gynt,* the onion that is the self, with its layers peeled off to reveal at the core nothing—this image has little reality for Furnivall, but it is an image that may be seriously thought of as the obsession of our own time.

With the twentieth century comes the renewed emphasis on the idea of the mask, the persona of classical drama; but now, as anticipated by Keats, the mask is a lyric as well as a dramatic conception. Whether by coincidence or not, the two men most closely associated with this development met in London in the first decade of the twentieth century and helped confirm in each other the importance of the concept that had captured their imagination. Of Yeats, we need not say a great deal here. This is in part because the doctrine of the mask has already

7. William K. Wimsatt, Jr., and Cleanth Brooks, *Literary Criticism: A Short History* (New York: Knopf, 1964), p. 537.

been treated in exhaustive detail by Yeats's critics, but also because Yeats's use of the mask is far less startling in its application than Pound's. For Yeats, the mask is the objective face chosen by the knight of subjectivity, the poet, that he might make himself and his works known. The mask helps provide the coldness in Yeats's notion of a poem "cold and passionate as the dawn."[8] To be sure, Yeats demonstrates his awareness of the arbitrariness of the mask, and, in the poem "The Mask," the corollary that since the mask is all we have it must be granted authenticity. But this is stolid stuff indeed if we compare it to the uses to which Pound is about to put the mask.

First, Pound actually gives to the body of his important work before the *Cantos* the name *Personae*, that is, masks. And much of that work is in fact an attempt to see the world through modes of apprehension used by those of his predecessors considered by Pound worthy of emulation. "The Seafarer," for example, reproduces in a modern idiom the sensibility of an Anglo-Saxon bard, "Na Audiart" that of a Provençal troubador. Not an unusual way for the novice poet to learn his art. But Pound discovered that the wearing of masks was not simply a way to learn one's trade, not simply a way to disguise oneself— but a legitimate means of expression. At what precise moment he discovered this it is difficult to say, but it is clear that he had learned his lesson by the time he wrote "Hugh Selwyn Mauberley" (1919–20).

"Mauberley" operates, in part, by allusion. In the first of its eighteen poems, for example, Mauberley is compared to or represented by Ronsard, Capaneus, Odysseus, and François Villon. This is on the border of mask, but hardly unknown in English poetry. But then Pound proceeds to write poems about Dante Gabriel Rossetti, Victor Gustave Plarr, Mr. Brennbaum (Max Beerbohm?), the acolyte of a corrupt editor, an unnamed "stylist," a bank-clerkly Englishman, the prize of a literary salon: and all these are Mauberley.

8. *The Collected Poems of William Butler Yeats* (New York: Macmillan, 1956), p. 146.

Like allusion, the use of masks draws attention to similarities among apparently unrelated characters, thereby shedding light, we hope, on both vehicle and tenor of this kind of metaphor. But masks go beyond this. Personality is fragmented. Versions of Mauberley, who is, after all, himself an invention of the poet, are as important as Mauberley himself. And Mauberley is nothing if not a version of Pound. In the past, in James, for example, we have assumed, if not the integrity of the outer world, at least the integrity of the self. However, as Whitehead and others will remind us, reality lies neither in the observer nor in the thing observed. Therefore, consistency of personality is no longer any more significant than constancy of objective reality. It is the relationship between the two that must remain consistent if it is to be representative of a given reality; and, in "Mauberley," it is precisely that relationship, and that relationship alone, that remains consistent.

I have already suggested that the mask is an intermediate step between the subjectivity of center of consciousness and the final abandonment of ego as arbiter of experience. A world of interrelated subjectivities, made possible by giving up the idea of the uniqueness of the self and of its separation from all other selves, becomes not only a new way of expressing the individual's sense of reality, but also a new way of conceiving it. So that Pound, seeking to explore implications of his life and work until that point, and to speculate about possible new directions, chooses a series of masks rather than analytic introspection.

It has been suggested that "Mauberley" is actually a poem about Henry James. And although it seems clear that "Mauberley" is primarily a comment on Pound's own life, or rather on what Pound thought his life might very well turn out to be if he did not leave England, the allusion to Henry James may nonetheless be appropriate. Mauberley's chief fault, the one that destroys him, is his subjectivity. For the poem is not simply an attack on the modern world and its attitudes toward the artist. It is in addition to that an attack on Mauberley's way of dealing with that world. He retreats from the struggle, withdraws into his private citadel, and passes out of existence. Quite possibly, this is the way Pound saw his fellow expatriate James. But he also decided that his own art would avoid those traps. He would find a base that was both subjective and objective at the same time, a base that, in fact, obliterated such distinctions.

To recapitulate: The loss of faith in an objectively knowable universe leads to the taking of a self-consciously subjective position by the artist. (We have been talking of literature, but the same process is evident in the development of Impressionism in painting.) Similarly, the loss of faith in the coherent, consistent personality, leads to the adoption of the mask as a legitimate means of self-expression. Finally, the use of a variety of masks simultaneously, or at least in rapid succession within the same work makes possible a stance that is neither objective nor subjective. (The analogous development in painting is, of course, the multiple planes of Cubism.) However, as in the sciences there is a relationship between theory and technology, in poetry there is a relationship between stance and technique. By the time he wrote "Mauberley," Pound had already made the major breakthroughs that proved crucial to his most significant work.

The next chapter will be devoted to an examination of the methodology Pound helped develop. However, that methodology, as we shall see, represents only one of the possible responses to the new sense of the self. Imagism, Objectivism, and Projectivism are chiefly concerned with the perceptual universe, with the self's relation to outer reality. However, there are other poets, the Confessional poets, for example, who are more interested in breaking down the barriers of the self in an inner direction. In a sense, the difference in emphasis we observe here is the same as the difference between Marshall McLuhan, who is concerned with how media make us perceive the world, and Norman Brown, who is concerned with making conscious much that is now repressed. However, I hope to demonstrate that, as in the case of McLuhan and Brown, these poets are responding to the same new sense of reality, that they are not striking out, as superficially seems the case, in unrelated directions, but are actually part of the same general phenomenon.

CHAPTER THREE

Poetry for a Discontinuous Universe

IT has for some time been evident that Imagism was crucial to the development of twentieth-century poetry. But although Ezra Pound is generally associated with the movement's propagation, and although he finally emerged as its chief spokesman, the origins of what has been called "modern poetry in miniature"[1] are far from clear. Noel Stock speculates that the basic Imagist principles emerged from a discussion among Pound, Hilda Doolittle, and Richard Aldington in April 1912, and that Pound applied the term *Les Imagistes* to writers governed by those principles either at that very meeting or within a month of it;[2] and that is certainly as precise as a discussion concerned more with theory than history need be. However, it is important for our purposes to realize that the vision of reality implicit in the movement belonged to no particular individual. It was based on ideas that had already begun to excite men's minds, ideas whose implications were available to those who could perceive them.

In fact, in 1909, when Pound was still too thoroughly immersed in the literatures of the past to take much notice, T. E. Hulme was writing of the "visual concrete" language of poetry. "Images in verse are not mere decoration, but the very essence

1. *The Imagist Poem: Modern Poetry in Miniature*, ed. William Pratt (New York: Dutton, 1963).
2. Noel Stock, *The Life of Ezra Pound* (New York: Pantheon, 1970), p. 115.

of an intuitive language."[3] Hulme, with his fondness for metaphysical systems (especially Bergson's), had become the intellectual and theoretical focus of a new group of somewhat rebellious poets that included F. S. Flint, Edward Storer, Florence Farr, and, later that year, Pound himself.

In August 1911, after spending a little over a year back in America and on the continent, Pound returned to London. But now what Hulme had to say was of the greatest importance, since it was paralleling, if not inspiring, his own thought. Much of what Hulme was saying has been collected in the posthumously published *Speculations* (1924), a book that contains many of the underpinnings of Imagism. Most well-known is the essay "Classicism and Romanticism," in which Hulme characterizes Romanticism as "spilt religion," pointing out that the attempt to compete with religion leads poetry into the abstract and infinite instead of its proper domain, the concrete and finite. It is time, he insists, for a "period of dry, hard, classical verse. . . . It is essential to prove that beauty lies in small, dry things."[4] It is, of course, the Image that meets his specifications. In addition, although here he may sound at least somewhat romantic himself, Hulme emphasizes the organic nature of the poem, helping to provide a theoretical justification for free verse.

However, it is actually in an essay that is rarely cited in relation to modern poetics, "Humanism and the Religious Attitude," that Hulme discusses the real core of his vision, the metaphysical perception that makes necessary the shift in emphasis he proposes.

> We constantly tend to think that the discontinuities in nature are only apparent, and that a fuller investigation would reveal the underlying continuity. This shrinking from a *gap* or jump in nature has developed to a degree which paralyses any objective perception, and prejudices our seeing things as they really are. For an objective view of reality we must make use both of the categories of continuity and discontinuity. Our principal concern then at the present

3. Stock, p. 65.
4. *Speculations* (New York: Harcourt Brace, 1936), pp. 133, 131.

moment should be the re-establishment of the temper or disposition of mind which can look at a *gap* or chasm without shuddering. (*Speculations,* pp. 3–4)

We shall soon be involved in a fuller discussion of the implications of discontinuity. For the moment it will be sufficient briefly to point out the connection between Hulme's metaphysics and his poetics. It is precisely the Romantic notion of personality, which Hulme would abandon in favor of the objective perspective, that imposes continuity upon the discontinuous universe. The conscious self formulates abstractions that make of reality a coherent whole. Hulme does not deny the legitimacy of such efforts, any more than he denies the legitimacy of philosophy or theology, but he does implicitly consign to poetry the business of recording human perceptions. He proclaims the new emphasis of twentieth-century poetry, the shift to the epistemological.

But it would still not be accurate to credit Hulme with the founding of the Imagist movement. Hilda Doolittle, for example, was more instrumental in giving significant poetic form to ideas that Hulme could only turn into a distinctly minor poetry. And Pound himself, in 1938, decided that Ford Madox Ford (then Hueffer) was "The critical LIGHT during the years immediately pre-war in London" rather than Hulme.[5] It was, in fact, Ford who announced that it was poetry's job to put "one thing in juxtaposition with the other" as "such juxtapositions suggest emotions,"[6] thus outlining the method by which Hulme's gaps could become the basis of poetic form.

Imagism, then, was a collaborative effort. Although it is of scholarly interest to determine who contributed which specific principles, it is more important for our purposes to recognize that the development of Imagism was a product of cultural imagination. For in addition to Pound, Hulme, Ford, and H. D., such writers as F. S. Flint, Richard Aldington, Amy Lowell, John Gould Fletcher, William Carlos Williams, and D. H.

5. Quoted in Hugh Kenner, *The Poetry of Ezra Pound* (Norfolk, Conn.: New Directions, 1951), p. 307.
6. Quoted in Stock, p. 137.

Lawrence were numbered among the first Imagists. More important, almost every significant poet growing to maturity at this
time, including T. S. Eliot, Wallace Stevens, Marianne Moore,
and e. e. cummings, was at one time or another an Imagist (although, as we shall see, most ultimately went beyond its limitations). Even prose writers were influenced (or did some in-
fluencing), for example, James Joyce (who appeared in *Des
Imagistes,* the first Imagist anthology, in 1914), Gertrude Stein,
and Ernest Hemingway. In fact, so thoroughly have Imagist
principles permeated the contemporary critical sensibility, they
are scarcely recognized as the bias which, of course, they are.

The popularity of Imagism has never seemed mysterious. In
one sense, it is simply a reaction to Romanticism, or at least to
the excesses of Romanticism, as they manifested themselves in
the Victorian and, most particularly, Decadent periods of the
nineteenth century, in the same way that Romanticism itself
can so profitably be seen as a reaction to Neo-classicism. However, even if the inevitability of such a reaction seems from our
perspective evident, it is still worth asking why the reaction took
this particular form. Why, for example, was a "classical" movement heralded by what is, superficially at least, a further breakdown in form? Why is the judgmental, rational side of the poet,
always important during classical periods, given so little weight?
To understand these paradoxes, it is necessary to examine in
detail the implications of Imagist principles. And we may find
that the incessant appeals for form and for order which abound
on the surface of Imagist doctrine are a consequence of the intuitive realization that form and order in the traditional senses
of those words are no longer possible.

The basic tenets of Imagism have admittedly been thoroughly
examined by critics of Modernist poetry; but the movement has
not so often been taken seriously as the manifestation of a distinct mode of apprehending reality as opposed to a strictly technical revolution. The first Imagist manifesto appeared in *Poetry*
in 1913. It was written by Pound and F. S. Flint, and it is Flint's
three rules that constitute the most well-known definition of
Imagism.

1. Direct treatment of the "thing," whether subjective or objective.
2. To use absolutely no word that did not contribute to the presentation.
3. As regarding rhythm: to compose in sequence of the musical phrase, not in sequence of a metronome.[7]

Since *thing* may be either subjective or objective, we are justified in understanding Flint to mean the experience being recorded, or the perception of an inner or outer reality. What is most important is that the poet must not talk *about* the perception, but rather create a structure that will allow the reader to experience it himself. This constitutes a rejection of the conscious intellect as a legitimate mediator of experience. The ego, instead of being asked to perform its traditional function of shaping reality, is being asked to step aside so that reality may be experienced directly.

The rejection of excessive verbiage is certainly an attack on the notion that poetry is adornment rather than condensation. It is also, by implication, a warning against the tendency to overinterpret experience, to endow it with qualities that are later additions to the initial perception. Since the ego cannot be totally eliminated from poetry, or else poetry would cease to exist, it must at least be discouraged from overextending itself.

In his preference for the musical phrase (free verse) as opposed to the metronome (metered verse), Flint gets to the heart of the argument. It is a question of what will give the poem its shape. The important characteristic of meter, for the purposes of this discussion, is that it exists as a rationally apprehensible construct in the poet's mind before the poem is written, in fact, before the experience that is the occasion of the poem exists. Of course, the poet has a choice of several meters (and stanzaic patterns) from which he may select the one most appropriate. But this is closely related to the logical process of classification; the categories already exist, reality must conform to them. This presents no problems as long as we have confidence in the va-

7. J. P. Sullivan, ed., *Ezra Pound: A Critical Anthology* (Baltimore, Md.: Penguin, 1970), p. 40. Unless otherwise indicated, the Pound quotations are from this anthology, with page references given parenthetically in the text.

lidity of the categories, in the capacity of the intellect to manage them, and in the usefulness of the entire process. However, if we feel that we have, after all, been imposing a logical system on reality, distorting it rather than objectively describing it, we must find an alternative method of organizing experience. As a consequence, the most important statement about the nature of reality a poem can make is its form. Metered verse assumes that all human experience can be contained within the framework of a relatively small number of pre-existing forms, and with this assumption the Imagists disagree.

Pound, in "A Retrospect," puts it this way:

> I think there is a "fluid" as well as a solid content, that some poems may have form as a tree has form, some as water poured into a vase. That most symmetrical forms have certain uses. That a vast number of subjects cannot be precisely, and therefore not properly rendered in symmetrical forms. (p. 84)

The vase, of course, is meter. Whatever you pour into it will take the same shape. The tree is free verse, and will take its shape from the particular circumstances in which it exists. But it *does* have form of its own. An oak is, after all, an oak, and cannot be an elm. And each individual tree has a growth appropriate to itself. Pound places on the poet the obligation to find the form appropriate to the particular experience. This was a touchy point for Imagists, and for most serious writers who followed in their footsteps. It led Pound repeatedly to quote Eliot's remark that "No *vers* is *libre* for the man who wants to do a good job" (p. 87). And it raises the very serious question of how the poet is going to know when he has found the right rhythm, the right form. This is simply another way of stating the difficult problem raised—and perhaps not dealt with—by Brown and McLuhan: granting the inadequacy of the conscious, rational ego in coming to terms with experience, what alternative do we have; if we find one, how will we judge its validity?

On this point Pound is not particularly helpful, not if we are looking for a scientific understanding of what he has in mind. "I believe in an 'absolute rhythm,' a rhythm, that is, in poetry which corresponds exactly to the emotions or shade of emotions to be expressed. A man's rhythm must be interpretive, it will be, therefore, in the end, his own, uncounterfeiting, uncounter-feitable" (p. 83). William Carlos Williams, Charles Olson, and Robert Duncan, locating the source of rhythm in biology, in breathing, heartbeat, and muscular system, may be of help in interpreting Pound's remarks. For the time being, we must be content to notice that whatever the source of "absolute rhythm," it will not be the conscious, rational ego. That is precisely why Pound finds it so difficult to talk about.

Before going on to Pound's own contribution to the original Imagist manifesto, there is another point to be considered. In insisting on free verse, the Imagists seem to be underestimating the complexities of meter. In fact, very few good poems conform precisely to any metrical pattern. The chief advantage of meter is that it sets up a sequence of expectations in the reader's mind, and the good poet can play skillfully with these expecta-tions, fulfilling them, for example, when he wishes to convey the impression of harmony, frustrating them when he wishes to suggest discord. The loss of this framework, this backdrop against which the poet can work out the tensions of his poem, is a severe blow. It helps account for the fervor with which Pound and his fellow practioners of free verse insisted on the difficul-ties of their art. They were aware of the subtleties of meter, and merely claimed comparable subtlety in their own work.

Pound admits that "symmetrical" form has its uses. But he does not seem to think those uses have anything to do with his own experience. For after his apprenticeship, during which he experimented with the most intricate forms imaginable, and was especially attracted by the more torturous Provençal forms—it was Arnaut Daniel, the most ingenious of all, he most admired—Pound abandoned formal verse, except for purposes of irony as in "Hugh Selwyn Mauberley." And the Objectivist and Projectivist poets, heirs to Imagism and the *Cantos,* have abandoned it altogether. The clear implication is that while pre-vious ages may have found symmetrical form appropriate, ours cannot. And while it is certainly accurate to say that modern ex-perience seems to preclude symmetrical form, that in itself may be merely the symptom of a more nearly fundamental phenomenon: while previous ages have had confidence in the ability of intellect to shape experience, ours does not. After Freud, Einstein, and Heisenberg, we must find some other mode of recording and communicating our perceptions of reality.

Pound begins his section of "Imagisme" with a definition which, while it has its difficulties, has the merit of approaching the poem from a point of view distinct from Flint's. He will not only comment on *how* the Imagist poem is written, he will tell us *what* it does as well.

> An "Image" is that which presents an intellectual and emotional complex in an instant of time. I use the term "complex" rather in the technical sense employed by the newer psychologists, such as Hart, though we might not agree absolutely in our application.
>
> It is the presentation of such a "complex" instantaneously which gives us that sense of sudden liberation; that sense of freedom from time and space limits; that sense of sudden growth, which we experience in the presence of the greatest works of art. (pp. 42–43)

Complementary to Flint's insistence on "direct" treatment, Pound's emphasis is on the instantaneity of presentation. The poet does not sequentially or analytically unfold his perception; he communicates it holistically—Hart is one of the early Gestalt psychologists—in a moment that is almost out of time, certainly out of time as a specifically human construct. We could say that the Image is the response of the total organism, rather than simply its mind, to experience.

Pound's definition of the Image is in many ways close to what we have come to think of as the Symbol. And this point requires some clarification. Pound most emphatically contended that "Imagisme is not symbolism" (p. 49). But this distinction was based on his understanding that the French Symbolists were engaged in allegory, or at least in allusion of a precise sort. It is probably irrelevant to remark that Pound is mistaken in his interpretation of the Symbolists. But it is quite relevant to take a standard definition of the Symbol, like the one developed by William York Tindall for his book *The Literary Symbol,* and compare that to Pound's "Imagisme."

The literary symbol, an analogy for something unstated, consists of an articulation of verbal elements that, going beyond reference and the limits of discourse, embodies and offers a complex of feeling and thought. Not necessarily an image, this analogical embodiment may also be a rhythm, a juxtaposition, an action, a proposition, a structure, or a poem. One half of this peculiar analogy is what it symbolizes.[8]

The similarity in terminology—"a complex of feeling and thought" as compared to "an intellectual and emotional complex"—can hardly be accidental. Tindall was thinking of Pound. What is important, however, is that the Symbol is close enough to the Image to make this association reasonable. The Image and the Symbol have in common the quality of eluding the boundaries of specific reference and of rational discourse. Nonetheless, beyond the fact that something other than an image may be the concrete manifestation of a Symbol, Symbolism and Imagism differ significantly. While both may be distinguished from a metaphor in that they are not compared to any particular object or idea, the Symbol is still being compared to something, no matter how indefinite or multifaceted that something might be. The Symbol is part of an unstated, or rather an unstatable, analogy. But an analogy itself implies a system of intellectually affirmed connections. The Image seems to involve simply the act of perception; it is a question of seeing rather than of understanding. And though a perception may in itself bring news of the universe, that news cannot merely not be dissociated from the perception, it is indistinguishable from that perception. The complex of meaning of the Symbol is similarly bound to its concrete form, but rather as soul is for Yeats bound to a dying animal. Image is the animal itself, albeit an animal that does not think of itself as dying.

It is possible to conclude from the attempts at definition we have to this point examined that the Imagist poem is a serious project whose goal is the representation of "objective" reality. The very name of the movement seems to suggest emphasis on perception of the outer world. However, that same word implies

8. Bloomington: Indiana University Press, 1960, pp. 12–13.

an observer, and Pound is quite explicit in rejecting the idea
that poetry should be the description of what exists outside, and
independent, of the poet. "Don't be descriptive; remember that
the painter can describe a landscape much better than you can,
and that he has to know a deal more about it" (p. 43). It was
probably the ease with which the term Imagism could be made
to mean poetry that painted pretty pictures in free verse (as well
as the struggle for proprietorship of a new movement) that led
Pound to denounce the work championed by Amy Lowell, calling it *Amygisme,* and to declare himself a Vorticist.

In his essay "Vorticism" (1914), Pound, in addition to placing
his specifically poetic movement in the larger context of a revolution of all the arts, more or less restates basic Imagist principles. But he also makes two significant additions to his original
manifesto. First, he draws attention to the poem as an energetic
construct, as something that is active rather than passive. "The
Image is not an idea. It is a radiant node or cluster; it is what I
can, and must perforce, call a VORTEX, from which, and through
which, and into which ideas are constantly rushing" (p. 56). Although we can detect here an almost desperate wish to make it
clear that what he is doing is not what Amy Lowell is doing,
Pound is also pointing out a characteristic of the new poetry
easily overlooked, one that takes on added importance in the
light of later pronouncements by Williams and Olson concerning the poem's "energy." It reminds us, in any case, that whatever the drawbacks of the absence of clear, logical structures,
the new poetry stirs things up, creates motion.

The second new contribution, which helps explain the first, is
Pound's description of the process of writing an Imagist poem.
The poem is the familiar "In a Station of the Metro":

> *The apparition of these faces in the crowd;*
> *Petals on a wet, black bough.* [9]

Pound tells us what inspired the poem: "Three years ago in
Paris I got out of a 'métro' train at La Concorde, and saw sud-

9. *Personae* (New Directions, 1949), p. 109.

denly a beautiful face, and then another and another, and then
a beautiful child's face, and then another beautiful woman
. . ." (p. 51). True to his principles, Pound does not try to make
the poem "descriptive." As vague as the prose may be, it is far
more precise than the poem itself. The poet is trying to capture
the impact the scene had on him rather than the scene itself.
"In a poem of this sort one is trying to record the precise instant
when a thing outward and objective transforms itself, or darts
into a thing inward and subjective" (p. 34). It is the moment of
perception that Pound is after, the interface between inner and
outer worlds.

Pound, having decided against longer, more elaborate attempts to capture the experience, describes how the desired effect is to be achieved. "The 'one-image poem' is a form of super-
position, that is to say it is one idea set on top of another" (p.
53). As is frequently the case with Pound, he has managed to
get to the heart of what he is talking about, but left the edges
blurred, so blurred that the center itself is in danger of being
obscured. First, we may notice that by definition the "one-image
poem" is in fact a two- (or more) image poem. There cannot
exist a "one-image poem" since the Imagist poem operates by
means of the relation of images. Second, what Pound calls
"super-position" should more properly be called juxtaposition,
since, whatever Pound's intent, the poem exists in time, and, as
a matter of fact, it is precisely because the two images can be
placed side by side that the poem works. And finally, we can see
that what Pound means by "idea" in this essay would more accurately be rendered by perception or fantasy, for that, rather
than ideas, is what the poem consists of.

Nonetheless, in context, the point is clear. The poet communicates his perception of reality by the juxtaposition of
images drawn from inner and outer realities. Interestingly, the
"apparition," the outer world, is less vivid than the "petals," the
inner world. But in any case, the "meaning" of the poem resides
neither in one realm or the other, but rather in the gap between
them. And this gap, the gap anticipated by Hulme and Ford, is
the crucial and original contribution of Imagism.

In the examples of Haiku Pound uses to explain what he has done in the "métro" poem, Pound supplies the words "are like" for clarity, thus transforming juxtaposition into more familiar simile. This is strange, because it is only by the omission of those words that the poem has any claim to literary significance. We should, to illustrate this, compare the actual poem with the following hypothetical poem:

> *The apparition of these faces in the crowd*
> *Is like petals on a wet, black bough.*

The rhythm, of course, has been thrown off. But let us assume that the poet could solve that problem. The real difference involves the relation of images.

The hypothetical poem is a sentence; the real poem consists of two fragments. The use of proper syntax asserts the ability of the conscious mind to form significant relationships between perceptions or imaginings. This is precisely the case in metaphor or simile, where the poet in effect says, "we all know that the areas of experience I am comparing are not identical, but they have something in common; so let us agree to notice the comparison and not the contrast, which we can do because our intellects are capable of selecting or abstracting from reality relationships that are not immediately evident." But without the proper use of syntax, the poet is proposing neither comparison nor contrast. He is simply saying, "here are two areas of experience that I associate with one another; let them play against each other, without prejudice as to their relationship, because if you do you will probably experience something similar to what I experienced when I was inspired to write this poem." And we are, in fact, left free to notice the contrasts between the images as well as the similarities. Or, to put it more accurately, we are invited to feel what it is like to be aware of the nearly simultaneous existence of both of these images, since to compare and contrast is a function of intellect, while the juxtaposition of images is a function of perception, involving not only intellect, but the sensory apparatus as well.

An obvious consequence of this technique is the reader's increased participation in the creative process. As Stanley Burnshaw suggests, the reader's involvement in the poem is not a modern development; it is, in fact, one of the defining characteristics of poetry. For poetry is the response of the total organism to experience, and that which is non-conscious in the reader has always assisted in achieving the poem's effect. However, in the past the poem has been characterized by a rationally comprehensible surface, on which necessary connections have been made by the poet, thus providing a focus for the reader's attention. In Pound, the surface is no longer available, or rather it no longer performs the same function. A useful analogy with painting can be made. It is perfectly conceivable that in any painting, whether it be by Botticelli, or Rembrandt, or Velásquez, the aesthetic effect has been achieved by relations of form, color, and texture. But in those representational works, the intellect can relate to objects drawn from conscious human experience, and can fit those objects into its pre-existing understanding of reality. In abstract painting, form, color, and texture certainly do their job; but the representational surface is absent, and the viewer is left to deal with those aspects of reality that can be least effectively mastered by the intellect. The analogy cannot be pushed too far. Poetry, certainly Pound's poetry, is by necessity representational; words have meanings, even phonemes suggest them. And Pound is passionately concerned with ideas. But he does not make connections among those ideas. He often frustrates the attempt of the intellect to organize them into recognizable patterns. But the very attempt to form those patterns draws the reader into the poem.

There is another way to express this involvement of the reader, a way, based on an analogy drawn from Marshall McLuhan, which has the advantage of directly relating the effect under discussion to its underlying causes. McLuhan distinguishes between the cinema, where the eye focuses on the screen (or rather, as we shall see shortly, just in front of it), and television, where the focus is in the eye itself, thus accounting for the greater participation of the viewer of television, the greater passivity of the viewer of a movie.

With TV, the viewer is the screen. . . . . The film image offers many more millions of data per second, and the viewer does not have to make the same drastic reduction of items to form his impression. He tends to accept the full image as a package deal. In contrast, the viewer of the TV mosaic, with technical control of the image, refigures the dots into an abstract work of art on the pattern of a Seurat or Roualt.[10]

We can think of the dots as the images juxtaposed by Pound to produce the Imagist poem. But more important, the distinction between film and television is related by McLuhan to the distinction between literate and nonliterate man; that is, between man having a fixed point of view from which he can rationally organize experience and man having "instant sensory awareness of the whole" (p. 28). In other words, the increased participation of the reader may well be related to the diminished power of the ego to provide a fixed point from which reality can be rationally shaped.

So familiar are we now with the basic tenets of Imagist poetry, with the possibilities of stark juxtaposition as opposed to logical connectedness, that it is easy to overlook the importance of Pound's innovations. In fact, their importance can scarcely be overstated. The problem was how directly to communicate experience rather than talk about it. The solution was to by-pass the assumptions about reality inherent in the structure of our language. That one should wish to bypass the insights available to us through the use of sophisticated language is in itself remarkable, and could only occur at a time when confidence in the intellect's capacity to master experience was at a low ebb. Pound, therefore, must avoid rational discourse, replacing abstraction with the concrete, replacing logical structure with bare juxtaposition. There is even an impulse, which admittedly does not take Pound too far, to do away with traditional written forms of language, in themselves abstract, and replace them with something more concrete. This accounts for his concern with Fenollosa and the Chinese ideogram, which he understood to form definitions by juxtapositions of concrete qualities rather

10. *Understanding Media* (New York: New American Library, 1964), pp. 272–73.

than by abstraction. We might further speculate—making use of another of McLuhan's principles—that Pound was attracted by the synthetic character of the ideogram, built up by combining particular qualities into a unique whole, as opposed to the analytic alphabet, which breaks reality down into interchangeable component parts. In short, we are linking the changes in technique proposed by Imagism to a far broader change in sensibility, in perceiving the world, in understanding the nature of the self.

That the Imagist revolution should be seen in purely technical terms is perfectly comprehensible. It is necessary, perhaps even advantageous, to give whatever we encounter a familiar shape. But a work like Pound's *Cantos* will accept no familiar shape, and should be an indication to us that something is amiss, for that poem, which is constructed along Imagistic principles, or rather an extension of those principles, has presented almost insurmountable problems for literary critics. The critic who examines the *Cantos* as if it were put together by traditional methods is in the position of either struggling against all evidence to assert that the poem is in fact unified in the conventional sense of the word, or deciding that, in spite of its passage of undisputed power and beauty, it is at best fragments of or notes toward a complete poem, and is, in its present state, a magnificent failure. I would like to explore the possibility that the *Cantos* is neither of these things, that it is, for better or worse, a poem that implies an approach to reality not readily accessible to conventional criticism, since that criticism is itself based on a view of reality that the poem rejects.

The two significant ways in which the *Cantos* differ from traditional poetry are, first, in its treatment of time, and, second, in its lack of a fixed point of view. These two characteristics are linked together by necessity rather than accident; both are functions of the traditional ego, of literate man.

Although Pound uses historical materials throughout his poem, and although he is very much concerned with presenting his own theories of political and economic history, the methodology of the *Cantos* breaks down historical time. The most obvious means by which Pound achieves this effect is by eschewing chronological sequence. The poem consists of fragments drawn from history, literature, mythology, and the poet's personal experience. The very fact that each of these sources evokes a different sense of time, with mythology out of time altogether, would make the development of a chronology difficult, since Pound does not subordinate any areas of experience to a dominant one, but rather allows them to exist without any sense of contradiction. This is distinct from the method used by James Joyce in *Ulysses,* where conflicting time schemes are subordinated to the carefully worked out chronology of Bloomsday, so a sense of real time remains. Moreover, even when it is possible, Pound does not observe sequence within any given area of experience. Or rather the question of sequence does not come up, since Pound is not unfolding stories, but referring to the same events, either repetitiously or from different perspectives. This should be distinguished from the methodology of Faulkner's *The Sound and the Fury,* in which time has been thrown into varying degrees of disorder. In Faulkner's book, however, fragments nonrepetitiously describe discrete moments in time, and the reader could, if he wished, rearrange the novel so that it follows perfect chronological sequence (although, as Jean-Paul Sartre has pointed out, that would make it a totally different book). No such rearrangement would be possible in the *Cantos.* In effect, more completely than either Joyce or Faulkner, Pound moves in space rather than time.

A second technique used by Pound is the conflation of episodes that are conventionally located at separate moments in time so that they take place simultaneously. This is precisely what Joyce does in *Finnegans Wake.* But instead of playing with individual words and phrases to develop simultaneous levels of meaning, Pound uses continuing metamorphosis, as in Canto IV, where Itys and Cabestan interchangeably are murdered and fed to a loved one, where Actaeon and Peire Vidal simultaneously run through the forest as animals. Or Pound may combine the literary sensibilities of various cultures and periods, as in Canto I, where he presents Odysseus' descent into the Underworld by Homer, as translated into Latin by a Renaissance author, translated by Pound himself into modern English, with a verse pattern derived from Anglo-Saxon poetry.

Although Pound's treatment of time is, as I have suggested, in some ways even more extreme than that of such contemporaries as Joyce and Faulkner, it is nonetheless important to this study to recognize that all of these writers have joined the scientists in their assault on the notion of time as something objective and absolute, something that exists independent of the consciousness that perceives it or the circumstances of that perception. We might in this respect take note of the medieval paintings that depict various events in a religious story on a single canvas or panel; *sub specie aeternitatis* all time is present.

Or, to go back farther still, we might note that as far as the creation of a sense of time is concerned Pound seems closer to his great model, Homer, than to more recent literature. As Erich Auerbach has pointed out, Homer creates a foreground without background, a continual present,[11] and that is a reasonably accurate description of the mosaic that is the *Cantos*. In addition, Homer expands and contracts the sense of duration through the *Odyssey* in a way that brings to mind Henri Bergson. Finally, Homer mixes history, myth, fantasy, contemporary and archaic viewpoints in a way that would have offended most senses of decorum through the past few centuries. (That it did not is a consequence of ignorance—the veracity of the historical base, and the mixing of twelfth- and eighth- century realities of the *Odyssey* are comparatively recent discoveries.) McLuhan would unquestionably attribute these similarities to the fact that Homer was pre-literate, Pound post-literate. In any case, it is more than coincidence.

It is worth recalling at this point Norman Brown's contention that "repression generates historical time,"[12] and Marshall McLuhan's linking of sequence and continuity with literacy:

---

11. *Mimesis* (New York: Doubleday, 1957), pp. 2–3.
12. *Life Against Death* (New York: Random House, 1959), p. 103.

"The visual makes for the explicit, the uniform, and the sequential in painting, in poetry, in logic, history. The non-literate modes are implicit, simultaneous, and discontinuous."[13] In both Brown and McLuhan, there is a relationship between locating oneself in time and in space. In Brown, repression leads to historical time and to the spatial organization of the body. In McLuhan, the dominance of visual perceptions leads to sequence and to the fixed point of view. For both writers the very conception of a knowable universe is dependent on the discrete and detached observer, and is therefore itself under attack. The point is not, however, whether Brown or McLuhan's analyses are accurate, and certainly not that Pound consciously anticipated their theories. It is rather that Pound seriously questioned the exclusive validity of historical time as a mode of apprehending human experience, and that he did it when the sensibility that was to produce a Brown and a McLuhan was developing.

As we have already seen, the loss of confidence in the existence of an objectively knowable universe leads to the increased significance of the first-person narrative as an epistemological statement as opposed to a mere convenience, and to the development of the center of consciousness and the persona. This provides not only an intermediate theoretical step between reality as seen from a single omniscient perspective and as seen from multiple perspectives, but also provides the technique by means of which the latter approach to reality can be presented.

In one sense, the use of multiple perspectives is not at all unfamiliar, not at all difficult to grasp. The theory of archetypes gives us a perfectly comfortable way of understanding the technique. The hero, whether he be Odysseus, or Sigismundo Malatesta, or Mussolini, lives or relives essential human experiences. Even the fact that Pound uses a variety of voices in his presentation of these experiences presents no problem. It is simply a way of dramatizing the distinct modes through which universals may be expressed. There is every reason to believe that

13. *The Gutenberg Galaxy* (New York: New American Library, 1969), p. 73.

Pound himself had some such plan of organization in mind. In a letter to his father, in 1927, he wrote:

A. A. Live man goes down into world of dead.
C. B. The "repeat in history."
B. C. The "magic moment" or moment of metamorphosis, bust thru from quotidien into "divine or permanent world." Gods, etc.

(p. 93)

But although Pound intends to achieve unity in his long poem by means of definite patterns, any reader of the *Cantos* who has been jarred by rapid transitions in material and changes of voice at least suspects either that something unconventional is indeed happening, or that Pound is, at best, perverse, at worst, mad. For whatever abstract system Pound or the critic may devise, the experience of reading the poem denies ordinary attempts to unify its materials. The archetypal approach to literature insists that apparently diverse actions can be seen as manifestations of a single thematic reality; but Pound's poem maintains the separateness of its fragments at the same time that it suggests their relationship. This is disconcerting to the literate mind. It is only a question of emphasis, but that question turns out to be crucial.

First, let us examine a concrete instance of Pound's use of multiple perspective, an instance that goes beyond the theme of metamorphosis. One of the most well-known, and most often anthologized, parts of the poem is Canto XLV, the "Usury Canto," whose conclusion is reproduced here:

Usura rusteth the chisel
It rusteth the craft and the craftsman
It gnaweth the thread in the loom
None learneth to weave gold in her pattern;
Azure hath a canker by usura; cramoisi is unbroidered
Emerald findeth no Memling
Usura slayeth the child in the womb
It stayeth the young man's courting
It hath brought palsey to bed, lyeth
between the young bride and her bridegroom

CONTRA NATURAM

They have brought whores for Eleusis
Corpses are set to banquet
at behest of usura.[14]

At least part of the reason for the Canto's popularity is its comprehensibility. It is a polemic, an exhortation filled with biblical overtones, that operates rhetorically rather than through logic. It is an extravagant piece, overloaded with feeling unless one recognizes that for Pound usury is not simply an economic perversion, but a symbol of all perversions, "CONTRA NATURAM."

It may seem curious that Pound, in this Canto, is flying in the teeth of his own proscriptions. "The 'image' is the furthest possible remove from rhetoric. Rhetoric is the art of dressing up some unimportant matter so as to fool the audience for the time being. . . . Even Aristotle distinguishes between rhetoric, 'which is persuasion,' and the analytical examination of truth" (p. 48). Pound would certainly have believed in the underlying truth of his harrangue, and the imagery is at times striking. But the Canto is not analytic, it is intended to persuade, and the parallel sentences and phrases which gives the passage its strength are unquestionably rhetorical in nature.

The conclusion we should reach is not that Pound is repudiating his own principles, but rather that the methodology of the *Cantos* allows him—even demands—a wide range of voices and stances. Canto XLV presents Pound as prophet in an almost biblical sense; it is a public voice. It should be compared with the following selection from the less frequently quoted Canto LII.

———— *sin drawing vengeance, poor yitts paying for* ————
paying for a few big jews' vendetta on goyim. . . .
IGNORANCE, *sheer ignorance ov the natr ov money*
    sheer ignorance of credit and circulation.
Remarked Ben: better keep out the jews
    or yr/ grand children will curse you

14. *The Cantos of Ezra Pound* (New York: New Directions, 1970), p. 230.

jews, real jews, chazims, and neschek
also super-neschek or the international racket

(CANTOS, p. 257)

It is not difficult to imagine why this passage is less well-known. It is nastier, it raises the specter of Pound's anti-Semitism, which, like much of his ideology, is liable to give a sense of acute discomfort to the reader. In addition, this selection is less coherent. But the connection between the two selections is quite clear. *Neschek* is the Hebrew word for usury, which in both cases is a curse, maybe the curse, on mankind. The voice of Canto LII is private; it is one of Pound's intimate voices. And the temptation is to read the private voice as revealing the motivation of the public voice. Pound's anti-Semitism is then the cause of his obsession with usury, to which he might in any case object, but without locating it at the center of his vision of human evil.

In a sense, this reading is correct. And, rightly or wrongly, I do not seriously doubt that there is a close association between Pound's anti-Semitism and his economic theories. But we are dealing with a poem, not a person. And everything in the poem suggests that we should be reading these two passages not as two manifestations of the same impulse but rather as distinct views of the same problem, not linked together by cause and effect. The voices are certainly distinct. And the fact is, there is no single persona available to connect those voices. In order to make the connection, the reader must supply his own imagined persona. That he so willingly does this is simply habit; it is not justified by the poem. Of course, the reader knows that Pound is the author of both Cantos. Is he not then entitled to assume connections not explicitly made by the poem? That is simply begging the question. We are not involved in a denial of the existence of a self, but rather in the re-examination of what constitutes a self. In Pound that self is characterized by fragmentation rather than cohesiveness. More accurately, the *Cantos* rejects the notion that the self constitutes a single point of view.

In *The Gutenberg Galaxy,* Marshall McLuhan associates the maintenance of a single attitude or tone in literature with the development of the printing press.

> It was disturbing to scholars to discover in recent years that Chaucer's personal pronoun or his "poetic self" as a narrator was not a consistent *persona*. The "I" of medieval narrative did not provide a point of view so much as immediacy of effect. In the same way grammatical tenses and syntax were managed by medieval writers, not with an idea to sequence in time or space, but to indicate importance of stress. (p. 166)

McLuhan then quotes so respectable a Chaucerian as E. T. Donaldson distinguishing three separate Chaucers in the *Canterbury Tales*. In the *Cantos* there are innumerable distinct Pounds. To return, however, to the two Usury Cantos: if we accept the differences in voice, tone, and perspective, rather than try to rationalize them, we must conclude that the passages should be juxtaposed according to the principles of Imagism, not related causally according to the impulse to unify.

McLuhan, as a matter of fact, supplies several analogies by which the structure of Pound's poem can be clarified; they are all the more striking since McLuhan did not at all have Pound in mind. He cites, for example, Georg von Beksy's work on acoustic space. "The paradox presented by Professor von Beksey is that the two-dimensional mosaic is, in fact, a multi-dimensional world of interstructural resonance. It is the three-dimensional world of pictorial space that is, indeed, an abstract illusion built on the intense separation of the visual from the other senses" (*Gutenberg Galaxy,* pp. 56–57). In the analogy I wish to propose, the three-dimensional perspective, made possible by the fixed point of view, would allow us to see both Cantos as emanations, at different depths, of the same unifying node. The mosaic would force us to juxtapose the two Cantos without unifying them. The Cantos are a mosaic.

An alternative analogy makes the same point. *The Gutenberg Galaxy* contains excerpts from a paper by John Wilson describing his attempts to use a film to teach African natives how to remove standing water (pp. 48–50). The film showed the techniques involved in slow, painstaking detail, but when the natives were asked what they had seen, they replied that they had seen a chicken. Puzzled, the Europeans reran the film and discovered that a chicken had, in fact, appeared for a second, by accident. Further questioning revealed that the natives had also seen other discrete elements of the film, but that the one thing they had not seen was the entire screen at once. In order to see the entire screen, one must focus in front of it; if one focuses on the screen itself, one can see only the small part of the screen upon which the eye has focused. Focusing in front of the screen apparently comes "naturally" to literate man, but the non-literate natives had to be educated to cinematic conventions. Focusing in front is the consequence of a fixed point of view, of the ability to locate oneself unambiguously in time and space.

The conventional poem is intended to be experienced from a fixed point of view. The reader focuses "in front of the screen." As a result, he expects to apprehend the work as a whole, and expects the entire work to be unified. Every segment must relate to every other segment. In fact, we have learned to discredit everything in a poem that cannot be shown to be an inevitable part of the whole pattern. A corollary to this is that the poem forms a closed system. And the natives watching Wilson's film confirm this corollary by their inability to accept the fact that once a person had left the picture he no longer existed; they wanted to know what had happened to him and could not grasp the fact that he no longer had anything to do with the story. The closed system depends upon the fixed point of view.

The *Cantos* deprives the reader of the fixed point of view; they insist that he focus "on the screen." This is not to say that the elements of the *Cantos* bare no relation to each other. It is rather that the reader is frustrated in his attempts to perceive the work as a whole; he must experience it piece by piece. The archetypal patterns Pound writes of to his father are present, but they do not bear the entire weight of the poem's details. Deprived of a satisfactory intellectual framework, the reader is plunged directly into the experience. And this, of course, is precisely the goal of Imagism: direct treatment of the thing.

In addition, the *Cantos* forms an open system. Partly because it is in places too private clearly to be understood, partly because it is accidental (its contents dictated by the course of Pound's life rather than by any rigid central plan), the poem permits no sharp distinction between life and art; it does not recognize discrete intellectual constructs. Like closed poems, it too comes to an end; but it does so because its creator comes to an end rather than because it has been completed. Foreign to us, these are all characteristics that the natives who wanted to know what happened to the man after he left the screen would have understood perfectly.

The *Cantos*, then, is a mosaic of fragments drawn from a variety of modes of apprehending reality, set flatly side by side rather than arranged symmetrically in relation to a fixed point of view. Each fragment must be scanned individually and juxtaposed to immediately touching fragments, not placed at once in the context of a broad, generalized pattern. Unity must be achieved as a consequence of the perceptual act itself, each perception becoming a tentative attempt at ordering reality that is by nature temporary, that is valid only at the perceptual moment, rather than as a function of a consistent, logically derived system of which each particular changing component can be seen as part of a stable generality. In fact, the basic archetypal themes of the *Cantos*, the descent into and return from the Underworld, and the continuing process of metamorphosis, are themselves representations of the poet's own unending process of decreating and creating anew the observed universe.

This understanding of the methodology of the *Cantos* can be applied to a line by line reading of the work, to the relation of individual components, and to the apprehension of the poem as a whole. Let us first examine some individual lines, those which open Canto II. To make sense of these lines conventionally is more or less possible, but only with a great sense of strain, and without a feeling of having come to terms with what the poet is doing.

Hang it all, Robert Browning,
there can be but the one "Sordello."
But Sordello, and my Sordello?

Lo Sordels si fo di Mantovana.
So-shu churned in the sea.
Seal sports in the spray-whited circles of cliff-wash,
Sleek head, daughter of Lir,
          eyes of Picasso
Under black fur-hood, lithe daughter of Ocean;
And the wave runs in the beach-groove:
"Eleanor, ἑλέναυς and ἑλέπτολις!"
          And poor old Homer blind, blind as a bat,
Ear, ear for the sea-surge, murmur of old men's voices:
"Let her go back to the ships,
Back among Grecian faces, lest evil come on our own,
Evil and further evil, and a curse cursed on our children,
Moves, yes she moves like a goddess
And has the face of a god
          and the voice of Schoeney's daughters
And doom goes with her in walking,
Let her go back to the ships,
          back among Grecian voices.
And by the beach-run, Tyro,
          Twisted arms of the sea-god,
Lithe sinews of water, gripping her, cross-hold,
And the blue-gray glass of the wave tents them,
Glare azure of water, cold-welter, close cover. (CANTOS, p. 6)

We encounter first a reference to the Provençal poet Sordello, but a reference to Sordello turns out to be no simple matter. There should be just one Sordello, *the* Sordello; that is, our reason tells us that there is an objectively knowable universe out there, and we ought to know it. But reality exists only as a relationship between observer and observed. Accordingly, Robert Browning, whose monologues support the notion that reality is a function of consciousness, becomes the "muse" of the Canto, in a sense of the entire poem. So instead of one Sordello, we have Browning's Sordello, Pound's Sordello, the Sordello of a biography more nearly contemporary to the troubador, and possibly, by implication, Sordello himself, through his works. We

then encounter So-shu, either a philosopher or a poet, but in
any case, churning the sea, a man who attempts to give form to
flux. As the waves break, we see the daughter of an Irish sea
god; the eyes either of a painter or his painting; Helen of Troy,
destroyer of ships and cities; Atalanta, most of whose suitors
met their doom trying to marry her; a nymph raped by a sea
god; and then, after the almost sexual excitement of the opening rhythms, a relatively calm seascape.

What have we seen? The Protean nature of reality, constantly
shifting, constantly changing its shape, and the poet, like Odysseus, hanging on for dear life. The sea itself in endless motion;
in a sense, everything that we see in these lines is seen in the
waves of the sea. The violence of ocean. The destructive power
of beauty, the danger inherent in the attempt to see reality as it
is (or, as Rilke put it in his first Duino elegy, beauty is only the
beginning of terror that we can still just barely endure). Possibly a cubist's view of reality, endorsing the legitimacy of seeing
the world from multiple perspectives.

We can, in fact, relate these perceptions intellectually. The
one difficulty is to make the connection between sea as
destroyer and beautiful woman as destroyer, and even that can
be dealt with if we recognize the importance of Aphrodite, who
was born out of the waves of the ocean, and who, for Pound,
represents the creation of form out of flux, and who can be
identified with Helen and Atalanta. There is still a loose end or
two, but nothing serious. Just enough to preserve a sense of
rough edges. What has not been sufficiently noticed, however,
is the fact that there is no real need to make connections, since
the series of perceptions in themselves, unorganized, constitute
an apprehension of reality. It is not even necessary to understand all the allusions, since the sense of the sea's violent energy and beauty is not dependent on a clear grasp of each separate wave. In fact, to dwell too long on each reference is to
defeat the purpose of the passage, to slow it down. The critic
then becomes like a man watching a movie, and trying to understand images of a storm at sea by freezing motion and studying individual frames. To organize and relate the images ra-

tionally is to attempt to contain the sense of motion, of uncontrollable energy, so that what we are left with is the idea of what he is trying to do rather than the actual experience of it.

The juxtaposition of Cantos is similar to the juxtaposition of lines and images. Take, for example, Cantos XIII and XIV. In XIII, Kung, or Confucius, is the central figure. He is a principle of order. But it is significant that Pound chooses Confucius as opposed to any other orderly philosopher. Kung says, "If a man have not order within him / He cannot spread order about him" (*Cantos*, 59). Order is something that emanates from the individual; it is not an abstraction. And Confucius is one of the authors of the *I Ching*, whose guiding principle is that order must be understood in terms of continual change. But order, however flexible, is still order. Canto XIV, on the other hand, presents a vision of disorder, of unnaturalness, of perversion. It is the first of three "Hell Cantos." It is easy enough to interpret XIII as a vision of potential order and XIV as the disorder that actually prevails at the present time. But this is to underplay the relativity of order in the former Canto, and to ignore the implicit definitions of what would constitute an orderly society in the latter. We are still dealing with Protean reality, with two simultaneously valid perceptions rather than with alternatives. Whether reality appears orderly or chaotic is completely a matter of angle of vision. The Cantos are complementary rather than contradictory. They are not related sequentially, causally, or analytically. They are juxtaposed.

There are, then, alternative readings of the *Cantos* available that significantly alter critical emphases. However, while particular portions of the *Cantos* have provided annoying, minor problems, no single part of the poem presents overwhelming difficulties. But the *Cantos* as a whole has been harder to digest. I have already alluded to this impasse, but I would like at this point both to review the problems and refer to an articulate spokesman of the negative perspective. Noel Stock, Pound's biographer, concludes *Reading the Cantos* with these words:

> He does not write poems, but poetry. And if sometimes the importance to him of what he is doing in the *Cantos* (forging "a weapon"),

and the desire to get it done and to show that the universe is a coherent whole, generate a field of force which holds the parts
together, we ought to see this for what it is. It is not form, only the
urge towards form, or at most the primitive beginnings of it. The
Cantos, as a result, do not constitute a poem, but a disjointed series
of short poems, passages, lines and fragments, often of exceptional
beauty or interest, but uninformed, poetically or otherwise, by larger
purpose.[15]

Coming from a critic so generally sympathetic to Pound, this
judgment must be seriously considered. But in order to evaluate
Stock's conclusions, we must understand the assumptions on
which they are based.

> But until we are able to see some, at least, of the relations between
> the parts, such as it is possible to hold in the mind for logical analy-
> sis and development, we cannot speak of the work as coherent. . . .
> Logical connection is a minimum, not a maximum, barely enough
> by itself, but without which the other relationships tend to give way
> to non-poetic ambiguity or disappear completely. . . . Pound's is po-
> etry of surface. And unless the surface has continuity and the tone
> is strong, the unity suffers. (*Reading the Cantos,* pp. 1–2, 9)

Stock does a fine job applying his principles to the text. If his
premises are correct, then his conclusion is eminently reasonable. However, we are now in a position to recognize that
Stock's underlying assumption is of a fixed point of view. From
that fixed point of view we would be able logically to unify the
poem, we would be able to create the illusion of depth instead of
the flat surface of Pound's mosaic. But we have seen that logical
connections, and a sense of "depth," may be thought of as im-
positions on reality rather than necessary modes of apprehending experience.

Nonetheless, with all his reservations, Stock would accept an
alternate source of unity: tone, the strong, identifiable voice.
But Pound will not even give us that. He shifts perspectives, obsessions, even, it seems at times, purpose. His intuition of the
nature of the self breaks down its boundaries. But what the
critic finds unacceptable the psychologist has little difficulty

15. New York: Minerva Press, 1966, pp. 116–17.

with. Whatever Pound can imaginatively involve himself in, whoever he can identify with, become part of the fabric of his poem. And he is free to link these fragments together in whatever order they occur, because their occurrence in that order is itself significant. And once we admit the possibility of the poet's self being expressed by a variety of voices and tones, we are free to recognize the underlying obsessiveness of his concerns. Whether he is wrapped up in Odysseus, Sigismundo Malatesta, Confucius, Adams, Jefferson, Van Buren, Mussolini, or his own experiences in a cage outside of Pisa, Pound is always involved in the attempt to give order to chaos. But he has set himself the formidable task of finding order without violating the chaos that is, after all, the real world. In the end, the poem is about itself, about its own creation.

The poem of a man who rejects the naive, if traditional, view of what a self is may possess unity, but that unity itself will necessarily be multifaceted. This appears to be a contradiction in terms. But if we will relax our prejudices, we will find that this conception of unity is not totally foreign to our experience. The problems that confront us in reading the *Cantos* are not very different from those emerging from our attempts to reconstruct a civilization that has left us some of its artifacts, some of its buildings, some of its literature. Say Greek civilization. We are fascinated by the challenge of trying to reconstruct the consciousness of a people who created the Parthenon, the Iliad, the statues and vases. We, in fact, succeed in achieving a certain degree of understanding. And yet, we are always uneasy about the rough edges of a "rational" society that behaved so irrationally in its political life, in the darker sides of its religious life. How can we reconcile Apollo with Dionysus; how can we even reconcile the Apollo who upholds rational law with the Apollo of ecstatic prophecy?

But if the ancient Greeks will not fit comfortably into any abstract pattern, they are nonetheless, in the fragments that remain of their civilization, a believable demonstration of how man relates to his universe. And this is precisely the kind of problem Pound leaves us with. Nor is it accidental that I have drawn on an entire society for my example. Not that Pound, even in his encyclopedic poem, is necessarily the representative of his society; but by identifying with as many aspects of that society, including its historical and cultural foundations, as he can, he becomes in effect *a* society in himself, contradictory, alogical, many-faceted, and yet possessed of an underlying unity of vision.

So we are drawn through the poem, piece by piece, continually called upon to reconcile the irreconcilable, denied the opportunity to organize the whole by means of any logical construct, but nonetheless invited to recognize a human being's attempt to make sense of his experience. This attempt cannot succeed if by success we mean a formula that can be abstracted from the whole (and that is generally what we mean, certainly what Noel Stock means). In a universe in which all truth must be relative truth, in which the attempt to observe reality is altered by the act of observation, both "truth" and "reality" must be redefined. Stasis in motion is what Pound offers us. And we have been asking for stasis, plain and simple. We will not get it.

Like his *Cantos,* Pound's stature as a poet has been subject to frequent attack. What is less uncertain, however, is his influence on contemporary writers, for here we are not dealing with critical judgment, which is, after all, fallible, but fact. And the fact is that Ezra Pound is probably the most influential—though this is not to say the best—writer of the twentieth century in English. Most of the poetry being written in America today, for example, in sheer quantity if not in academic approval, is written in the tradition developed by Pound, which forces us to admit, whatever our evaluation of Pound's own work, that it is in some sense responsive to our particular apprehension of reality. And of all the writers influenced by Pound, the one who is most important for purposes of our discussion—not because he slavishly follows Pound but rather because, in so many significant respects, he is so different—is William Carlos Williams.

On one point, at least, Williams was in perfect agreement with Pound. Imagism was a far more demanding discipline than most of its would-be practitioners recognized. In a popular sense, it had been successful in ridding poetry of excess verbiage. But in that same popular sense the Imagist poem had, in the hands of Amy Lowell and others, become what Williams called "the bare image haphazardly presented in loose verse." Like Pound and Eliot, he considered free verse a misnomer, an excuse for writing poems that lacked formal necessity. But form had been the essence of Imagism, the embodiment of its vision of reality. So in 1931, along with Charles Reznikoff and George Oppen, he created the Objectivist theory of the poem (and, later, the short-lived Objectivist Press). They argued that "the poem, like every other form of art, is an object, an object that in itself formally presents its case and its meaning by the very form it assumes."[16]

In one sense, Objectivism is simply an extension of Imagism, or rather an attempt to recapture its original principles. It is a reaffirmation of Pound's ideas, and shares Pound's distaste for the watering down of those ideas. By emphasizing the existence of the poem as an object in its own right, Williams, in addition to insisting on form, reinforces Pound's notion that the poem should not be descriptive, not dependent on an outer world that it slavishly imitates. And the very use of the term Objectivist implies objectivity of a sort, as opposed to the subjective, personality-rooted vision.

However, Williams is rather stingy with his remarks about Objectivism, and for an understanding of the details of his poetic theories, and their full relationship to Pound's, we can do no better than to turn to the prose sections of *Spring and All* (1923). Although this is, of course, an earlier work, it most clearly contains the theoretical underpinnings of Objectivism.

Near the beginning of *Spring and All*, Williams identifies the moment of perception as the terrain of the poem. The reader, he says, is at home in the past and in the future. "But the thing he never knows and never dares to know is what he is at the exact

16. *The Autobiography of William Carlos Williams* (New York: New Directions, 1967), pp. 265, 267.

moment that he is. And this moment is the only thing in which
I am at all interested."[17] This is closely related to the Imagist
tenet, "direct treatment of the thing." The poet will not talk
around the experience, he will not relate it to the past or future,
that is, to any abstract system that explains reality and to which
each individual component must be linked; he will present the
"now," the experience itself. But he is more explicit than
Pound—and this is characteristic of Williams—in making his
aesthetic principles a function of existential awareness. The intellectual apparatus, which constitutes most of what we commonly call the self, locates us in the past or future. We cannot
think about the present, because as soon as we think about it, it
has become part of the past. However, we can *experience* the
present, and this is the business of the poem. The present is,
after all, the only moment in which we exist; the poet's job is to
make us aware of that moment.

In short, far more openly than Pound, Williams is at war with
the traditional self. He wishes to enlarge it, and warns of the
dangers involved in narrowness of vision

> The inevitable flux of the seeing eye toward measuring itself by the
> world it inhabits can only result in crushing humiliation unless the
> individual raise himself to some approximate co-extension with the
> universe. This is possible by the aid of the imagination. Only
> through the agency of this force can a man feel himself moved
> largely with sympathetic pulses at work. . . . (p. 105)

We are reminded of man's dual existence. He is, as Burnshaw
points out, both a distinct consciousness, separate from the rest
of creation and acutely aware of that separation, and a harmonious part of nature, at one with the universe. By relating to intellectual constructs abstracted from reality rather than to reality
itself, man protects himself—at least that is one way in which
he protects himself—from the anxiety both of his aloneness and
the tenuousness of his separate existence. But for Williams, the
poet's task is to experience his real existence, without the props

17. *Imaginations* (New York: New Directions, 1971), p. 89. Page references
hereafter given parenthetically in the text.

ordinarily available. So he must bring into play the totality of his being, including much that is ordinarily repressed, and he can do this only by means of his imagination. With that imagination he can recognize the underlying identity of "pulses" within himself and in the world at large. What these pulses are, Williams does not specify. But we will probably not be far wrong if we suppose they are in some way connected with the universal rhythms described by Burnshaw.

Williams himself provides evidence to support this view: "In the composition, the artist does exactly what every eye must do with life, fix the particular with the universality of his own personality—Taught by the largeness of his imagination to feel every form which he sees moving within himself, he must prove the truth of this by expression" (p. 105). In asking the poet to "fix the particular with the universality of his own personality," Williams reverses the usual formula. We think generally of the particularity of the poet reaching out for the universality of experience, but here the poet must search within himself for the universal. According to the two passages quoted above, Williams clearly means that the poet perceives himself as part of the universe by locating that which is universal within him, and then, with the aid of the imagination, recognizes these universals in the world around him.

Williams' theory is put to practice in the first poem of *Spring and All,* "By the road to the contagious hospital" (pp. 95–96). The poem begins by establishing the specifically human world—in the words "road" and "hospital"—as a point of reference. "Road" appears again in a few lines, and it is the last sign of man as a distinct entity in the poem. First we *see* the plants,

> *the reddish*
> *purplish, forked, upstanding, twiggy*
> *stuff of bushes and small trees. . . .*

Increasingly, the imagery becomes tactile; the plants "enter the new world naked, / cold. . . ." And finally, at the poem's conclusion, "'rooted / they grip down and begin to awaken."

It is important for us to recognize precisely what Williams has done in this poem. He has not, for example, anthropomorphized the plants, attributing to them specifically human character-istics that they do not possess. He has rather searched within himself to find those human qualities that are a part of the total-ity of nature, imaginatively raising himself to some approximate coextension with the universe. Indeed, with the "standing water" (suggesting amniotic fluid), the purplish appearance of the plants (suggesting a woman's genitals before birth), and the fact that the plants enter the new world naked, the process of human birth is superimposed upon the annual rebirth of spring, emphasizing the underlying identity of human and natural worlds.

Williams, then, has extended Pound's theory of the Image. The poet bypasses—or plays down—intellect in favor of percep-tion because it is through the perceptual apparatus that the to-tality of the human being, including his participation in being at large, can be expressed. But we must be sure to notice that this constitutes an extension of, rather than a break with, Pound. In a poem like "By the road to the contagious hospital," Williams' purpose is "To perfect the ability to record at the Moment when the consciousness is enlarged by the sympathies and the unity of understanding which the imagination gives, to practice skill in recording the force moving, then to know it, in the largeness of its proportions—" (p. 120). This sounds very much like that "sudden liberation," "that sense of sudden growth, which we experience in the presence of the greatest works of art," which Pound uses to characterize the Image. It also sounds like the at-tempt "to record the precise instant when a thing outward and objective transforms itself, or darts into a thing inward and sub-jective," that Pound makes in the "Métro" poem. For both poets, the domain of the poem is the point of intersection between inner and outer realities. And in Williams, if not in Pound—at least not explicitly—the emphasis is on the identity rather than the distinctness of those realities.

However, precisely what kind of identity Williams has in mind is not immediately evident. Even in the poem referred to above, the tension between the human world and the rest of nature is present, even if only to be reduced to minor significance. And the act of imagination that raises man to an approximate coextension with the universe cannot be a mere copying of what is perceived without, but rather a new creation made in the same spirit as the original. "Nature is the hint to composition not because it is familiar to us and therefore terms we apply to it have a least common denominator quality which gives them currency—but because it possesses the quality of independent existence, of reality which we feel in ourselves. It is not opposed to art but apposed to it" (p. 121). What man shares with the rest of the universe is the fact of being. Man is also different from the rest of the universe; he is conscious being. But Williams is suggesting that the similarity outweighs the difference, that it is at the same time a source of comfort and a means of imaginatively transcending the helplessness and isolation of the human condition. So that in imitating nature, not by holding a mirror up to it but by himself becoming a creator of form, the poet explores and expresses his particular mode of being and its place in the larger scheme of things.

The method by which the poet operates is juxtaposition. Williams refuses to grant the "outer" world more reality than the "inner." Therefore, art and nature are not conflicting versions of a single objectivity reality, but rather independent realities that shed light on each other. Like Pound, Williams has abandoned the fixed point of view, from which reality must be hierarchically and sequentially ordered, and replaces it by mosaic, by apposition. Again, he has gone a step further than Pound. For while Pound sees the poem as composed of appositions of images, Williams sees the poem as a whole as part of a greater apposition.

We are returned to the theory of gaps. The universe is discontinuous, and the attempts of the conscious intellect to eliminate those gaps must ultimately fail. Knowing is, therefore, not a function of reason, but a perception.

> Imagination is not to avoid reality, nor is it description nor an evocation of objects or situations, it is to say that poetry does not tamper

with the world but moves it—It affirms reality most powerfully and
therefore, since reality needs no personal support but exists free
from human action, as proven by science in the indestructibility of
matter and of force, it creates a new object, a play, a dance which is
not a mirror up to nature but—

   As birds' wings beat the solid air without which none could fly so
words freed by the imagination affirm reality by their flight.
(pp. 149–50)

The crucial contrast, that between tampering and moving, is
not defined by Williams. But the context makes his remarks accessible. To tamper with the world must surely mean to change
it, to subject what is really there to interpretation. "The object
would be it seems to make poetry a pure art, like music" (p.
150). To explain is to alter the thing explained by the very act of
explaining, just as, in science, the object of observation is altered by the very act of observing. To move the world, as in the
analogy of the wings and air, is to juxtapose separate realities,
which confirm and elucidate each other's existence, not by explanation, but by the simple fact of proximity.

   The most explicit illustration of this theory of poetry is the
poem generally called "The Red Wheelbarrow."

   so much depends
   upon

   a red wheel
   barrow

   glazed with rain
   water

   beside the white
   chickens   (p. 138)

The poem begins almost as a logical proposition, but it can only
be completed by the bare juxtaposition of objects that follows, in
the manner of a sentence that begins with words and ends in a
pictograph. More can be said about the poem than is at first ap-

parent. It operates by contrasts of red and white, man-made and natural, inanimate and animate, shiny and dull, and so on, creating the illusion of an endless series of characteristics which depend on their opposites for definition. But ultimately the poem is about itself, since its own existence depends upon the contrasts of objects, and since it itself is an object juxtaposed to nature.

Admittedly, most of Williams' poetry is not as purely Imagistic or Objectivistic as "The Red Wheelbarrow." Some of his poems, like "To Elsie" ("The pure products of America / go crazy"), approach discursiveness, even seem to have a message (pp. 131–33). But even here the underlying principles are the same. "To Elsie," for example, operates not through sequential narrative or description, but by juxtaposed relationships. The limits of Elsie's imagination are measured by cheap jewelry, and then juxtaposed to the futile—or at least fleeting—escapes of our own imagination. The very occasion of the poem, the placing of Elsie in the home of a middleclass doctor, is juxtaposition. The unit of the Image has here been so expanded that we might well question whether or not it can still be called an Image— which is, in fact, often the case in Pound's *Cantos*—but the means of connecting one part of the poem to the other remains basically the same. Elsie's situation is elucidated not by analysis, but by placing it side by side with another situation. For Williams has limited faith in the dissections of analysis as a mode of knowing the world. Anticipating McLuhan's idea of a global village, he says, "In any civilized society everyone should know EVERYTHING there is to know about life at once and always" (p. 139). In the place of sequence and analysis is instantaneity and simultaneity. And the literary form appropriate to this way of knowing is the Imagist or Objectivist poem. Traditional knowledge, Williams leaves to prose. Poetry is "new form dealt with as a reality in itself" (p. 137).

With this theory of poetry, Williams encountered the same kind of difficulty as Pound in attempting to construct a comprehensive vision of reality. For we are accustomed to expressing comprehensive visions in terms of generalizations and logical structures. But the Imagist-Objectivist poem discourages both generalization and logic. It throws us back on raw experience, primarily because raw experience, or at least knowledge of raw experience, can no longer be taken for granted. But if the poet can not abstract a system of order from what he experiences, he cannot escape the order inherent in his arrangement of images. Just as the traditional conception of the self has been redefined rather than replaced, form is not being eradicated but rather rebuilt along lines more appropriate to the contemporary world.

Williams, however, is even more insistent than Pound on the formal values of his poetry. This insistence was indeed the chief rationale for the founding of Objectivism, and, later in his career, led him to invent the "variable foot," an uneasy compromise between free verse and formal meter. And this insistence also manifests itself in the organization of *Paterson*.

To begin with, *Paterson* had from the start what the *Cantos* had always to do without: a coherent plan. In *Paterson One*, Williams described the four books that were to constitute the poem: "Part One introduces the elemental character of the place. The Second Part comprises the modern replicas. Three will seek a language to make them vocal, and Four, the river below the falls, will be reminiscent of episodes—all that any one man may achieve in a lifetime." [18] There are other ways to express the poem's organization—perhaps better ways. The point is, it has an organization, and that organization preceded the writing of the poem. This pre-existing plan would seem incompatible with the notion that the poet's ego, his conscious self, is unable adequately to organize experience. And that, of course, is precisely the case. The content of the poem itself, as we shall see, argues against this version of form. And the poem won:

> [since completing *Paterson Four*] I have come to understand not only that many changes have occurred in me and in the world, but I have been forced to recognize that there can be no end to such a story I have envisioned with the terms I had laid down for myself. I had to take the world of Paterson into a new dimension if I wanted

18. *Paterson* (New York: New Directions, 1963), p. 7.

to give it imaginative validity. Yet I wanted to keep it whole, as it is
to me. (*Paterson,* pp. 7–8)

Williams has still not relinquished his conscious desire for
form, for wholeness. And, in a sense, he never did. But this
poem, like the *Cantos,* will not allow itself to be finished. Williams alludes to changes that have taken place in the world and
in himself, but these are not the crucial reasons for continuing.
He does not spell out "the terms I had laid down for myself,"
and it might not help much if he had. We must be reminded,
however, of the African native's curiosity about the men who
walked off the screen. As an Objectivist poet, Williams possesses the same curiosity, and for reasons that are related to
those of the natives, if not identical with them. The poet's job is
not to rationalize experience but to perceive it. And perceptions
will not conform to any rigid plan, no matter how comprehensive its author might have imagined it; they will not come to an
end until the perceiver does. So that the very existence of a plan
for the poem, by its frustration, becomes the chief argument for
the proposition that a poem written according to Williams' aesthetic principles could not have such a plan. When he died in
1961, Williams had begun work on *Paterson Six.*

Williams' greater concern with wholeness leads to another
distinction between his method and Pound's. Williams finds for
his poem a specific location, the city of Paterson and its en-
virons. He abandons Pound's attempt to turn time into space,
thus losing the opportunity implicitly to assert, as Pound did,
that in a sense everyone can be said to be in all places at all
times. Williams does, in fact, move back and forth in time. But
the span of time is relatively short, less than three hundred
years, compared to what Pound decided to work with. And the
present, or the near present, so dominates, that it becomes a
point of reference more fixed and precise than anything in the
Cantos. Of course, by relating Paterson the man and Paterson
the city to their natural surroundings, Williams enters a timeless world that dwarf's Pound's. But it is precisely a *timeless*
world, which may indeed assert man's participation in a greater
whole, but does no more than assert it, and balks at the attempt

to prove—as Pound attempted—that historical time itself can be attacked and broken down.

On the other hand, Williams, by virtue of that very strategy, breaks new ground in the effort to communicate a new sense of the self. The inclusion of particular materials in the *Cantos* is ultimately justified by the fact that it appears in Pound's mind; there is no other significant criterion for inclusion. What appears in *Paterson* is ultimately justified by the fact that it relates to Paterson (with some exceptions that we shall soon consider). Place rather than poet is the criterion. Pound did not really read for the *Cantos;* the *Cantos* had to accommodate what he read. We can, however, imagine Williams doing research on the history of Paterson because that history had to be part of his poem. In other words, by identifying with the city, by making the doctor, the giant, and the city all part of one multifaceted character, Williams expands the limits of the ego so that it incorporates materials that previously would have been considered external to it.

Charles Olson elaborates the resulting contrast between Pound and Williams.

> Ez's epic solves problem by his ego: his single emotion breaks all down to his equals or inferiors (so far as I can see only two, possibly, are admitted, by him, to be his betters—Confucius, & Dante. Which assumption that there are intelligent men whom he can outtalk, is beautiful because it destroys historical time, and

> thus creates the methodology of the Cantos, viz, a space-field where, by inversion, though the material is all time material, he has driven through it so sharply by the beak of his ego, that, he has turned time into what we must have, space & its live air. . . .

> the primary contrast for our purposes is, BILL: his Pat is exact opposite of Ez's, that is, Bill HAS an emotional system which is capable of extensions & comprehensions the ego-system . . . is not. Yet

> by making his substance historical of one city (the Joyce deal), Bill completely licks himself, lets time roll him under as Ez does not. . . .[19]

19. *Selected Writings of Charles Olson,* ed. Robert Creeley (New York: New Directions, 1951), pp. 81–83.

Olson's comments are of special interest since, as the first and principal theorist of Projectivism, he is the obvious heir to the tradition created by Pound and Williams; if he is not necessarily infallible as an interpreter of his antecedents, he is at least a legitimate spokesman for the movement they helped develop. Pound, says Olson, solves the problem of defeating time, but he can only do that by giving presence to the past in so far as it exists in his own consciousness. So that in spite of Pound's ability to speak with a multiplicity of voices, his own personality is inevitably stamped on the poem as a whole; in a sense, he has not escaped the limitations of his ego (although, we may feel compelled to add, he surely reshapes our notion of what an ego is). Williams, however, by choosing a place as repository of historical memory, creates at least the illusion of a consciousness that is generally rather than particularly human. But Paterson itself is subject to time, as are its inhabitants. Or, to put it another way, as far as the impact on the reader is concerned, time can only be broken down when it is directly confronted.

Pound and Williams, then, as Olson himself suggests, each solve one half of the problem. Pound can transcend time but not ego, Williams ego but not time. Whether it is in fact possible to eliminate both ego and time from the reality of the poem is a question we must reserve for further discussion.

Olson's remarks point out another distinction between Williams' methods of organization and Pound's: "the Joyce deal." Just as Humphrey Chimpdon Earwicker is both a specific resident of Dublin and the city itself, so Paterson is both Dr. Paterson and the city in which he lives. However, *Finnegans Wake* resembles the *Cantos* in its attempt to capture encyclopedically the materials out of which our culture has been constructed, while *Paterson* is happily provincial, as if convinced that the common pattern of human life prevails in all times and in all places, and that to absorb the totality of what has preceded us threatens to destroy the reality of where we are. Joyce occupies the middle of the continuum of which Pound and Williams constitute the extremes. Pound assumes no collective consciousness (or unconsciousness), but does give to his fragmented notion of the self the power to move freely in time and space; Joyce creates a collective mind that participates in the eternity of the unconscious, but he cannot conceive of it existing independent of place; Williams gives all importance to place, so that collective experience for him must include nature, and time is not so much rejected as perceived as partaking of the eternity of that natural world. In all three cases, the position of the individual, coherent consciousness as the chief interpreter of experience has been challenged.

The content of *Paterson* reinforces the challenge to the individual consciousness, to intellect, suggested by its form. The opening lines of the Preface—"Rigor of beauty is the quest. But how will you find beauty when it is locked in the mind past all remonstrance?"[20]—identify poetry's enemy: the mind. Man's dilemma in trying to understand the world and his place in it is that the very act of understanding, of abstracting from reality, is distortion. No matter how brilliant the insight, as soon as it has been expressed in rational terms, it becomes rigid, dead, removed from the experience it is trying to represent. It becomes, in fact, the cliché, the close-minded assumption about the nature of reality that must be destroyed so that reality can be directly perceived. Williams' method of dealing with this problem is

> *To make a start*
> *out of particulars*
> *and make them general, rolling*
> *up the sum, by defective means—* (PATERSON, p. 11)

The poet will avoid the problem of distortion through abstraction by an accumulation of concrete details; or, as he says a few pages later, "no ideas but in things" (p. 14). However, even this method is "defective":

> *For the beginning is assuredly*
> *the end—since we know nothing, pure*

20. *Paterson,* p. 11.

> *and simple, beyond*
> *our own complexities.*   (p. 11–12)

The phrase in apposition, "pure and simple," is ambiguous, since we cannot tell whether what we cannot know is that which is pure and simple, or whether we can simply know nothing at all. In either case, our complexities, the mind and the sensory apparatus, prevent an objective picture of reality. We are left with nothing but the perceptual act.

But a series of perceptual acts, represented through language, are converted by the mind into a new kind of abstraction, a new orthodoxy.

> *(The multiple seed,*
> *packed tight with detail, soured,*
> *is lost in the flux and the mind, . . .*   (p. 12)

Any kind of sure knowledge, even if it is expressed in terms of details, creates its own dogma, which by its very nature cannot remain true to the flux of experience. It is only the eye which, like that of Wallace Stevens' Snow Man, sees "nothing that is not there and the nothing that is"[21] that can know the world.

> *. . . In ignorance*
> *a certain knowledge and knowledge,*
> *undispersed, its own undoing.*   (PATERSON, p. 12)

Again, there is ambiguity. Does ignorance provide a certain kind of knowledge, or does it provide sure knowledge, which would then turn on itself? At first, it may seem strange to encounter a great number of Empsonian ambiguities in an Objectivist poet who has chosen to do business with things rather than ideas. But Williams has decided to prevent his craft from being "subverted by thought" (*Paterson*, p. 13) by giving thought full play. Consequently, *Paterson's* basic structure consists of alternate

---

21. *The Collected Poems of Wallace Stevens* (New York: Knopf, 1961), p. 10.

passages of abstraction and concrete detail. The propensity of intellect to dominate is undermined by the ambiguities themselves and by the juxtaposition to the concrete. On the other hand, the rolling up of details, that "defective means," is kept dispersed by the intruding abstractions, avoiding the self-inclosed "multiple seed." It is the tension between two imperfect ways of representing reality, the interpenetration between them, that makes available to the poem its field of action.

Carried to its logical conclusion, Williams' position rejects not only intellectual knowledge but even art in so far as it becomes a rigid representation of the flux that constitutes experience. And Williams does not flinch from these implications. In *Paterson Three,* the library burns, and the poet, although ambivalent, understands that in one sense he is on the side of the flames. For writing itself is "a fire, / a destroying fire," and "beauty is / a defiance of authority" (pp. 137, 144).

Paradoxically, the library, the repository of the world's great writing, stifles art, or at least its continued creation. "The library is desolation, it has a smell of its own / of stagnation and death . . ." (p. 123). This accounts for the most obvious distinction between the *Cantos* and *Paterson.* While the former is, in part, a fragmented library, the latter is very sparing of quotations. For Pound, the literary tradition can take root and flower in one's own consciousness, and can be legitimately used to break down the rigidity of the mind; for Williams, the literary tradition remains the product of other consciousnesses—however liberating the original act of creation may have been—and therefore is in itself a check to the imagination. In Williams' aesthetic, even the poet's own work must be put aside to make possible renewed creativity. "The province of the poem is the world" (p. 122), where it is alive, not the library, where it has begun to die or is already dead.

And yet, we must persist in calling a paradox this rejection of the past so that the world may be continually recreated in the poem. In *Paterson Five,* Williams does seem to suggest that art alone provides escape from death. Returning to the Unicorn tapestries at the Cloisters in New York City, which, in a more metropolitan notion of unity of place, he had mentioned earlier, Williams explicitly links the work of art with transcendence of temporality.

> *Through this hole*
> *at the bottom of the cavern*
> *of death, the imagination*
> *escapes intact*   (p. 247)

In fact, when he says that nothing is real but the paint squeezed from the tube by Jackson Pollack (pp. 248–49), the poet asserts the "higher" reality of art. *Paterson Five* is filled with allusions to artists: Gertrude Stein, Paul Klee, Durer, Leonardo, Bosch, Picasso, Juan Gris, Beethoven, Peter Brueghel. It is almost as if one of the important reasons for the writing of the fifth book was to give art its due, after having so seriously threatened its prominence. Even in this book, however, the emphasis is on the exercise of the imagination rather than its product. Williams concludes *Paterson Five* by reasserting the importance of formal values in poetry, in life. And his final metaphor puts in perspective the significance of art in human experience.

> *We know nothing and can know nothing*
> > *but*
> *the dance, to dance to a measure*
> *contrapuntally,*
> > > *Satirically, the tragic foot.*   (p. 278)

Art is a formal mode of conducting one's life; the imagination is shape. It is a "beautiful thing" juxtaposed to the chaos of matter. But it is also ephemeral. The dance, the art form that Williams chooses to stand for all art forms is inseparable from the artist, a way of conducting life rather than something detachable from life. And it is an art form that most obviously involves the entire organism.

While some of the differences between Pound and Williams

are crucial, they are clearly allies in the attempt to redefine the self. Pound emphasizes the continued existence in the consciousness of each individual of the civilized traditions that have helped shape his own culture, while Williams emphasizes the necessity of each individual recreating the world. Williams is concerned with man's participation in the totality of being, especially that aspect of it we conventionally call "nature," while Pound, generally less preoccupied with nature, anthropomorphizes it through the medium of myth instead of identifying with its qualities. Pound's view of reality lends itself to fragmentation, while Williams' can be expressed through relatively coherent wholes. Pound's concerns are more public, but he is more personal in his treatment of public materials, and while Williams deals more with a world he has personally experienced, he depersonalizes that world. As Olson pointed out, Pound more successfully contronts the humanly imposed limitations of time, while Williams is more successful with those of the ego. But both writers approach reality through multiple perspectives rather than the fixed point of view. Both assemble their poems by juxtaposition rather than narrative sequence or logical structure. Both express their visions of reality as a series of perceptions (even if Williams' perceptions are themselves more extended and even, surprisingly, more intellectual than Pound's) rather than as a system that can be verified by and imposed upon experience.

Although Pound and Williams, through the methodology of their poems, initiate the attack on the traditional self, it is not until Charles Olson that this movement, which has now passed through its Imagist and Objectivist stages to become Projectivism, explicitly and self-consciously redefines the perspectives from which the artist can legitimately view reality. Probably the most influential poetic manifesto ever written—if we measure influence by the sheer quantity of poets afected—"Projective Verse" is Olson's most well-known essay. Like Flint in the original Imagist manifesto, Olson begins with three principles defining his poetic school.

(1) . . . the poem itself must, at all points, be a high energy-construct and, at all points, an energy-discharge. . . .

(2) . . . FORM IS NEVER MORE THAN AN EXTENSION OF CONTENT. . . .

(3) . . . ONE PERCEPTION MUST IMMEDIATELY AND DIRECTLY LEAD TO A FURTHER PERCEPTION. . . . one perception must must must MOVE, INSTANTER, ON ANOTHER![22]

Williams, in *Spring and All* referred to the imagination as a force, like electricity or steam,[23] and it is possible that Olson had those remarks in mind in his description of "field composition." However, he explicitly mentions Pound's insistence on the "musical phrase" as opposed to the metronome, as well as forces "just now beginning to be examined." So that although Olson does not elaborate on his first principle, it is not very difficult to understand his intent. The energy-discharge seems an apt description of the tension created by logical gaps, by juxtaposition. The rhythm of the poems, then, will not be expressible in rational terms, but will emerge as a response of the total organism to experience.

Therefore, the form of the poem will be intimately related to its content, since content, as the response of the consciousness to experience, is only part of the picture and must be related to the total response in which it participates.

Finally, each response, each perception, must be juxtaposed without any intervening materials or explanations to the next response. Olson's three rules—which he names kinetics, principle, and process respectively—are in fact aspects of one single insight, which may be summed up in the notion that the poem is, as Burnshaw said, the response of the total organism to experience, and that it must therefore take the form of that response directly, and without interpretation or rearranging by the intellect.

As for the act of composition itself, Olson sees two halves:

the HEAD, by way of the EAR, to the SYLLABLE
the HEART, by way of the BREATH, to the LINE[24]

22. *Selected Writings*, pp. 16–17.   23. *Imaginations*, p. 120.

24. *Selected Writings*, p. 19. Hereafter given in text as S.W., with page number.

Olson isolates rational consciousness and the non-conscious body as the two components of poetic expression; together they constitute the total organism. It is significant, in the light of Marshall McLuhan's work, that Olson picks the syllable rather than the word as the head's fundamental unit, emphasizing the mind's analytic powers, its ability to break expression down into a finite number of sounds that can be reassembled in endless combinations. The rhythm of the poem, however, is a function of bodily rhythm, and is not consciously determined. The presumption is clearly that mind and body will, when allowed, work together.

Like both Pound and Williams, Olson warns of the dangers of description. "The descriptive functions generally have to be watched, every second, in projective verse, because of their easiness, and thus their drain on the energy which composition by field allows into a poem" (*S.W.*, p. 20). The warning is still necessary because of the temptation to translate that which is unfamiliar and possibly new into that which is comfortably recognizable. Imagism, Objectivism, and Projectivism can all be translated into a simple emphasis on the concrete as opposed to the abstract, and that is certainly part of it. But a sharply juxtaposed series of perceptions with no fixed point of view is not the same as an attempt to reproduce a conventional painter's interpretation of reality, fixed point of view and all. And the energy Olson refers to in his warning is precisely the energy released by eliminating the coherent point of view.

In the second part of his essay, Olson presents the metaphysical basis of his aesthetic principles. This is more than either Pound or Williams do for us, and the passage is consequently worth quoting at length.

Objectism is the getting rid of the lyrical interference of the individual as ego, of the "subject" and his soul, that peculiar presumption by which western man has interposed himself between what he is as a creature of nature (with certain instructions to carry out) and those other creations of nature which we may, with no derogation, call objects. For a man himself is an object, whatever he may take to be his advantages, the more likely to recognize himself as such the

greater his advantages, particularly at that moment that he achieves
an humilitas sufficient to make him of use.

It comes to this: the use of a man, by himself and thus by others,
lies in how he conceives his relation to nature, that force to which
he owes his somewhat small existence. If he sprawl, he shall find
little to sing but himself, nature has such paradoxical ways, by way
of artificial forms outside himself. But if he stays inside himself, if
he is contained within his nature as he is participant in the larger
force, he will be able to listen, and his hearing through himself will
give him secrets objects share. (*S.W.,* pp. 24–25)

"Objectism," close but not identical to Williams' term, is Olson's name for the Imagist-Objectivist-Projectivist tradition; if
we can trust his reading of Pound and Williams, Olson's remarks should illuminate their work as well. Much of the quoted
passage sounds like Williams, and the spirit is indeed the same.
But that is all the more reason to note distinctions.

Olson is the first of the poets we have been considering to attack by name the traditional ego. Although such an attack is implicit in the rejection of subjectivity and of logical analysis,
Pound and Williams limit the thrust of their criticisms to specifically aesthetic matters, and do not go so far as to say that the
very possession of an ego is an impediment to full awareness of
reality. For Olson as for Norman Brown, poetry can be the
means by which man's sense of himself can be expanded; but
while Brown sees that expansion as being accomplished by
making conscious that which is now repressed, Olson looks to
identification with outer reality for the same result.

Where Williams calls the poem an object, Olson points out, in
addition, that man himself is an object. In a sense, each statement is a corollary of the other. The poem, for Williams, is the
product of the imaginative perception of the individual's participation in the universe. Olson identifies the basis of this identification as the objectness of both individual and universe. The
poem, therefore, an expression of that equivalence, must also be
an object. (Williams says that art is real in the same way that
nature is; Olson says that what the poet makes must "try to take
its place alongside the things of nature" —*S.W.,* p. 25.) This distinction between Olson and Williams goes to the heart of the

matter. Although they are in essential agreement as to the changes that must take place in poetry, Williams roots these changes in aesthetics, Olson roots them in human consciousness itself.

Williams warns that man risks "humiliation" unless he "raise himself to some approximate co-extension with the universe."[25] Olson talks of man's "somewhat small existence" in relation to nature, and, like Williams, suggests that the poet look within himself for intimations of his universality, his connections with the world at large. The projective act, then, is the poet's participation in the universe of objects, participation which is accomplished by projecting outward what the poet finds most deeply within himself.

What Olson is proposing seems to approach mysticism. However, although he at one point assures the reader that he is not afraid of that label, there is little in Olson's work that would support such an interpretation. In "Human Universe," a more conventional essay less influential among poets but with easier access to its logical bases, Olson offers further explanations of his methods. He rejects the ordinary use of language for reasons with which we are by now familiar: "Logos, or discourse, for example, has, in that time, so worked its abstractions into our concept and use of language that language's other function, speech, seems so in need of restoration that several of us go back to hieroglyphs or to ideograms to right the balance" (*S.W.*, pp. 53–54).

What the language of abstraction cannot grasp is the immediate moment of man's existence; it cannot express man's true relation to reality. "It is not sufficiently observed that logos, and the reason necessary to it, are only a stage which a man must master and not what they are taken to be, final discipline. Beyond them is direct perception and the contraries which dispose of argument. The harmony of the universe, and I include man, is not logical, or better, is post-logical, as is the order of any created thing" (*S.W.*, pp. 54–55). By de-emphasizing the in-

25. *Imaginations*, p. 89.

tellect, the rational center of man, his soul, and consequently giving greater importance to the act of perception, "you have gone so far as to imply that the skin itself, the meeting edge of man and external reality, is where all that matters does happen, that man and external reality are so involved with one another that, for man's purposes, they had better be taken as one" (*S.W.*, p. 60). Olson's by-passing of the ego, like that of Pound and Williams, is not a question of mysticism but rather of how man will relate to his world. And for Olson, agreeing with Brown and McLuhan, it a question of recapturing an energetic interaction between inner and outer worlds that has been repressed by the forms of our civilization.

Pound, Williams, Olson are all involved in the construction of a theory of poetry whose bases challenge the conventional notion of what constitutes a "self." However, only Olson, who probes deeper and more explicitly into those bases than the others, confronts the implications of that challenge. What will the new self be like? What will happen to personality, the observable manifestation of the other self? Olson's response is not to deny the existence of personality, but to question its isolation, to question the legitimacy of abstracting it from the complex of experience out of which it emerges.

> I am not able to satisfy myself that these so-called inner things are so separable from the objects, persons, events which are the content of them and by which man represents or re-enacts them despite the suck of symbol which has increased and increased since the great Greeks first promoted the idea of a transcendent world of forms. What I do see is that each man does make his own special selection from the phenomenal field, and it is thus that we begin to speak of personality, however I remain unaware that this particular act of individuation is peculiar to man. . . . (*S.W.*, pp. 60–61)

Even if we grant specialized selection from the phenomenal field, Olson goes on, we must recognize that that selection is an interaction rather than the independent functioning of a coherent self; there is no use "in thinking that the process by which man transposes phenomenon to his use is any more extricable from reception than reception itself is from the world" (*S.W.*, p.

61). Alluding to Heisenberg's Indeterminacy Principle, Olson rejects description and, implicitly, abstraction, as means of expressing that interchange. Therefore, personality, which depends upon description and abstraction, and has no distinct, tangible form, must, in its conventional form, also be rejected. The poem, then, becomes the only legitimate expression of experience. ". . . art is the only twin life has—its only valid metaphysic. Art does not seek to describe but to enact" (*S.W.,* p. 61).

Olson's principal theoretical contributions to our discussion are his recognition that the technical advances made by Pound and Williams were implicitly grounded in a more or less consistent view of man's relation to the universe, and the explicit elaboration of that relationship. As a consequence, Olson is in a position to make statements about the extent to which "objectism" has been practically successful in fulfilling the promise of its theory.

We have already seen part of Olson's evaluation of the areas of success and failure in the *Cantos* and *Paterson.* Pound breaks down time, but only with the emphatic use of his ego. Williams extends the ego but, in the process, "lets time roll him under." Each solves half of the problem, but in such a way as to make the other half unlikely—if not impossible—to be solved. Olson clearly endorses Pound's methodology; in this respect, Williams "contributes nothing, in fact, delays, deters, and hampers, by not having busted through the very problem which Ez has so brilliantly faced, & beat. . . ." Perceiving Pound's contribution as central to his work, Olson sets himself a task that is at the same time specific and difficult to comprehend: ". . . I am trying to see how to throw the materials I am interested in so that they take, with all impact of a correct methodology AND WITH THE ALTERNATIVE TO THE EGO-POSITION . . ." (*S. W.,* p. 83).

The chief problem raised by Olson's poetic theories, then, is the discovery of that alternative. It is a problem that loomed in the background from the moment that Pound decided that a long poem could be written without logical transitions, without a consistent center of focus. For that meant that something other than the conscious intellect would have at least part of the burden of perceiving the wholeness and continuity of the work. The failure of Pound or Williams to confront this difficulty has contributed to the critical confusion in interpreting and evaluating their major works. Olson, as we have seen, is very much aware of the implications of his methodology, but unfortunately, though he tells us we must search for an alternative, he says nothing of its nature. The best we can do is examine his own poetry for some indication of what he might have meant, with special reference to contrasts with Pound and Williams, who each managed only half the job.

In spite of Olson's suggestion that Williams represents a dead end, the *Maximus Poems,* at least superficially, bears greater resemblance to *Paterson* than to the *Cantos.* As *Paterson* is centered on one American locality, so *Maximus* is centered on Gloucester, Massachusetts. As Williams avoids dependence on allusions that demand an extensive literary background, so does Olson. But Olson's sense of place is not Williams'. While Paterson resides in his city, in fact, is his city, Maximus is an exile, writing letters to Gloucester. And although he does not make extensive reference to broad historical, mythological, and literary traditions in the way that Pound does, and often provides information in the manner of Williams, nonetheless, what references there are are not purely local; Gloucester is linked to other sea-going cities, and basic configurations such as the juxtaposition of land and ocean become generalized far more extensively than in *Paterson.* So that while the action of *Paterson* takes place in Paterson, and while that city is universal in the sense that it is City, Gloucester is ultimately a point of reference, a place that must be abandoned in order to be understood, but one with which the poet must communicate if he is to be understood.

Maximus is, of course, a persona that embodies much of Olson himself. He may also be the figure of the poet in general, or at least of man as maker.

That carpenter is much on my mind:
I think he was the first Maximus

Anyhow, he was the first to make things,
Not just live off nature [26]

Although he is in many ways tied to Gloucester, Maximus is contemptuous of the condition in which he finds it; his name for its social and political system is "pejorocracy" (*Maximus,* p. 3). But Olson is not primarily interested in polemics against the materialistic, bureaucratic, industrialized world in which he lives; these are merely symptomatic of a failure accurately to perceive the nature of reality. "Letter 6" begins by declaring, "polis is / eyes" (*Maximus,* p. 26). The fact that so few in the polis use their eyes is at the root of its corruption. Rejecting lifeless abstraction, especially when it takes the place of true perception, Olson insists

There are no hierarchies, no infinite, no such many
                                        as mass, there are only
eyes in all heads
to be looked out of   (MAXIMUS, p. 29)

In place of society's dead values, Olson presents a vision that suggests the degree to which modern literature is an extension of the Romantic movement.

there is no other issue than
the moment of
                    the pleasure of
                              this plum,
these things
which don't carry their end any further than
their reality in
themselves   (MAXIMUS, p. 42)

Our society, our intellect, lead us astray; reality is accurately perceived only by those who can penetrate the world's tangle, or those who have not yet been fully enmeshed in it. Of his daughter, Olson says:

26. *The Maximus Poems* (New York: Jargon/ Corinth Books, 1960), p. 31.

She wears her own face
as we do not,
until we cease to wear
the clouds
of all confusion,

of all confusers
who wear the false face
He never wore, Whose
is terrible. Is
perfection   (MAXIMUS, p. 88)

We may say again that Olson is more explicit than Pound or Williams in condemning the conventional, socialized ego. But Pound's insistence on direct treatment of experience rather than abstractions about experience and Williams' appeal for an approximate coextension with the universe at least imply Olson's position. If this is the alternative to the ego-position, Olson can hardly claim to have invented it, nor can he comfortably criticize his predecessors for having fallen short of it. So the *Maximus Poems* requires further investigation.

In organization it presents even greater problems than the *Cantos* or *Paterson*. The *Cantos* has its archetypal skeletons and the strength of its interlocked allusions. *Paterson* is—in its original conception—divided into four books, each with its own main emphasis. But *Maximus* simply rambles along, haranguing Gloucester, comparing it to islands like Nova Scotia, Newfoundland, and Sicily, or ancient ports, such as Tyre, giving fragments of its history, excerpting historical documents. It is really only in *Maximus Poems* IV, V, VI, the second published volume of the poems, that the peculiarities of Olson's emphases begin to unfold.

The excerpts from historical documents, as, for example, *"In the interleaved Almanacks for 1646 and 1647 of Danforth,"* begin to appear with increasing frequency. And a new kind of mythological reference provides the poem's general framework:

The sea was born of the earth without sweet union
of love Hesiod says

But that when she lay for heaven and she bare the
thing which encloses
every thing. Okeanos the one which all things are
and by which nothing
is anything but itself, measured so

screwing earth, in whom love lies which unnerves
the limbs and by its
heat floods the mind and all gods and men into
further nature [27]

The documents are noteworthy only because of their increased use. The mythological passage, however, should be compared with those of Pound. While Pound relies heavily on Ovid, whose *Metamorphoses* provides the most important background to the *Cantos,* Olson draws his scene from Hesiod (or, in other instances, from Norse mythology). The contrast is between mythology filtered through the wit and cynicism of a sophisticated society, and mythology in its more nearly primitive form. In other words, it is the distinction between prerational psychic experience rationalized and made manageable by conscious intellect, and that same experience just after it has first been given coherent form, with the rough edges still showing, the primal energies still nearly intact.

Olson concentrates on that which can be "objectively" perceived—the documents—and on the communal representation of the human unconscious—the primitive myths. In each case, he eludes the ego and as much as he can of what separates man from man, and seizes upon those aspects of experience that are least controlled by consciousness. This is recognizably Pound's technique—but it is the technique of a Pound who, for better or

27. "Maximus, from Dogtown—I" in *Maxiumus Poems* IV, V, VI (London: Cape Goliard Press, 1968), pages not numbered.

worse, is far more aware of the implications of what he is doing. Quotations from the documents are more extensive, mythology is less rationalized, personality is less distinct. The question remains, however, whether Olson has simply pushed a methodology initiated by Pound to its logical conclusion, or whether he has, in fact, succeeded in developing "an alternative to the ego-position."

The movement from Imagism to Objectivism to Projectivism—summarized by Olson in the term Objectism—has been characterized by an increasing awareness of the implications of poetic techniques. Pound often says he is doing one thing and does another; Williams pinpoints the movement's basis, a new relationship between the self and the world; Olson explicitly asserts a new version of the self, one that plays down the traditional role of consciousness. But our survey is not complete without adding a footnote provided by Robert Duncan.

In his essay "Notes on Poetics Regarding Olson's *Maximus*," Duncan reinterprets Pound's "logopoeia" as "not only a verbal manifestation, but a physiological manifestation." Taking this into account, he formulates his account of the genesis of the poem as follows:

> The coming into life of the child: first, that the breath-blood circulation be gaind, an interjection! the levels of the passions and inspiration in phrases; second, that focus be gaind, a substantive, the level of vision; and third, the complex of muscular pains that are included in taking hold and balancing, verbs, but more, the movement of the language, the level of the ear, the hand, and the foot. All these incorporated in measure.[28]

The organic metaphor, seeming to obscure, is itself telling; the poem is born the way a human being is born. In addition to sight and hearing, emphasized by Pound but always linked by poets to their art, Duncan identifies breath, heart beats, and the muscular-nervous system as sources of the poem's rhythm and structure. We have come a long way from Pound's notion of

28. *The Poetics of the New American Poetry*, ed. Donald M. Allen and Warren Tallman (New York: Grove Press, 1973), pp. 191–92.

absolute rhythm. Whether Duncan's analysis applies to Pound's own work may remain debatable, but as a commentary on Objectism, in the manner of the poems written under its influence, taking on an organic life of its own, it is certainly pertinent. And the one area of human experience conspicuously left out by Duncan is the life of the mind. Not that consciousness can be totally eliminated without, perhaps, destroying poetry. But Objectism most clearly repossesses the body as a significant participant in man's response to his universe, making it at least an equal partner with the mind in giving shape to experience.

CHAPTER FOUR

Testing the Boundaries of the Self

IN twentieth-century American poetry, the traditional boundaries of the self have come into question. Charles Olson, speaking for Objectism, calls the ego a peculiar interposition between man and the rest of creation, thus challenging the outer boundaries. But there are inner boundaries as well. The unconscious, by definition, is separate from the conscious self, upon which it may nonetheless exercise some force. Inaccessible to voluntary investigation, the unconscious is often perceived as an alien power; it is understood to strike a crucial blow against the vestiges of free will, as if to be motivated by the unconscious were to be moved by someone or something other than ourselves. This interpenetration between conscious and unconscious assured at the least some questioning of the boundaries ascribed to them; and no modern poets have done more to erode these boundaries than the Confessionals.

Before examining the contributions of Confessional poetry, it is necessary to recognize the problems raised by the very use of that term. We are not dealing with a movement like those comprising Objectism, replete with manifestos by its principal practitioners, acknowledgment of mutual influences, significant personal relationships, and even, at one point at least, a geographical center at Black Mountain. The work of the Confessionals is not dominated by a common methodology, a common theme (unless psychic pain in its diverse manifestations constitutes a common theme), or even what could accurately be called, in its narrowest sense, a common sensibility. Friendships and exchanges of ideas and criticism do not exceed what might be found in any random sampling of contemporary poets in general. And finally, the movement, if such it is, has the distinct disadvantage of having had its very existence recognized retroactively. M. L. Rosenthal, whose chapter on Robert Lowell, Sylvia Plath, Allen Ginsberg, Theodore Roethke, John Berryman, and Anne Sexton in *The New Poets* (1967) presents, with reservations, the case for grouping these poets under a single heading, first conceived of the term he would use after the appearance of Lowell's *Life Studies* in 1959. But by that time, Roethke had published all but his last book, Ginsberg had written *Kaddish*, and even Berryman had explored something of the Confessional mode in his *Sonnets*. And Rosenthal's own doubts as to whether the movement lasted much beyond the deaths of Roethke and Plath in 1963, suggest the emphemeral nature of Confessionalism.[1]

And yet, however we wish to categorize it, something happened. In 1958, Sylvia Plath and Anne Sexton met while attending a course taught by Robert Lowell at Boston University. They came under the influence of a poet generally recognized as one of the two or three best of the postwar generation just at the time he was discovering new directions in his own work. The effect of this influence is described by Sylvia Plath:

> I've been very excited by what I feel is the new breakthrough that came with, say, Robert Lowell's *Life-Studies*. This intense breakthrough into very serious, very emotional experience, which I feel has been partly taboo. Robert Lowell's poems about his experience in a mental hospital, for example, interest me very much. These peculiar private and taboo subjects I feel have been explored in recent American poetry—I think particularly of the poetess Anne Sexton, who writes about her experiences as a mother; as a mother who's had a nervous breakdown, as an extremely emotional and feeling young woman. And her poems are wonderfully craftsmanlike

---

1. *The New Poets* (New York: Oxford University Press, 1967), pp. 112–13.

poems, and yet they have a kind of emotional and psychological depth which I think is something perhaps quite new and exciting.[2]

Our first concern must be to discover more precisely the nature of the new areas of experience now made available to the poet.

To express one's emotional responses to personal experience can hardly be termed innovative. Poets who have written of love, for example, from Sappho and Catullus to the present, certainly have expressed their emotions in their poetry. But Plath speaks of areas that are both private and taboo. Sappho and Catullus do not write about feelings perceived by them as taboo. Nor is it clear that they write about areas of experience that are private in the modern sense of the word. In fact, it is possible that the distinction between private and public cannot legitimately be made until a much later period of Western culture, that it is a distinction intimately linked to the split between intellectual and emotional life, between spirit and matter, given its formal statement by Descartes in the seventeenth century. It is Eliot's dissociation of sensibility; it is McLuhan's Gutenberg Galaxy.

John Donne, writing in an era of altering consciousness, is probably one of the first poets to take seriously the notion of a private world. In "The Canonization," Donne counters the argument of his friend who has suggested that the poet is ruining his life for love by saying, "As well a well wrought urn becomes/ The greatest ashes, as half-acre tombes." The world of private experience chosen by the poet is as important as—if not more important than—his friend's public world. There is a similar juxtaposition of public and private worlds in a poem like Catullus' "Vivamus, mea Lesbia, atque amemus," in which the poet tells his beloved to ignore the household spies who will report their love to the world at large. However, Catullus and Lesbia inhabit the same world as the spies; they are not mutually exclusive. For Donne, subjective and objective realities *are* mutually exclusive; and they are equally legitimate.

The eighteenth century accepts the split, but for the most

2. Quoted in A. Alvarez, "Sylvia Plath." *Tri-Quarterly,* No. 7 (Fall 1966), p. 69.

part that which is public triumphs over that which is private. It is not until the Romantic movement of the early nineteenth century that the subjective and private begin to dominate. Wordsworth's *The Prelude,* for example, is one of the first attempts to create a spiritual autobiography of the poet rooted in the concrete details of an often private universe, as opposed to, say, Dante's shaping of the particulars of his life in the interests of the universal in the *Vita Nuova.* And *The Prelude* is, in a sense, "confessional." The ride in the stolen boat is as confessional as Augustine's account of stealing pears. However, if both of these incidents involve acts that are forbidden, they are still not taboo. The stealing of a boat, like the stealing of some pears, may be sinful; but these acts do not uncover dark secrets of the psyche, they do not constitute that descent into the underworld that seems almost a defining characteristic of modern Confessional poetry.

However, if Wordsworth does not enter terrific places of the mind, some of his contemporaries do. Byron, for example, feeds the torment of characters like Manfred with his sense of personal sin and damnation. But although Romantic demonic visions may be rooted in the passions of their creators, the expression of those visions is universal rather than particular; Prometheus and Faust may embody the inner lives of Shelley and Goethe, but they also mask those lives. Madness in these poems becomes not a sickness but a heroic ideal, the symbol of man's refusal passively to accept the limitations of the human condition. In fact, much of the energy of Romanticism is directed toward an attempt to alleviate the frustrations resulting from the domination of the subjective by the objective that characterized the eighteenth century. And this in turn led to the next extension of Romanticism, Symbolism.

After the dominance of public and materialistic realities in the eighteenth century, and of personal and emotional realities in the early nineteenth, the Symbolists, conspicuously flaunting the growing new science, begin the job of reintegrating a dissociated sensibility. Baudelaire's "Correspondences" (1857) is the most obvious instance of this endeavor. We are in a forest of symbols in which the natural world corresponds to the spiritual and the spiritual evokes the material. The subjective life of the human mind is linked to objective reality. The Symbolists did not, of course, discover the doctrine of correspondances. A line drawn from Hermes Trismegistus leads to such mystics as Jacob Boehme and Swedenborg, who in turn inspired Vaughan, Traherne, Blake, and Yeats. In America, the Transcendentalists found the natural world a book of spiritual truth. Hawthorne, Emerson, and Melville knew it as well as Hermes: as above, so below. Nonetheless, the Symbolists' concern with the doctrine of correspondance in its special context, that is, as an answer to the frustrations generated by Romanticism's emphasis on the subjective, may in itself constitute a "new" doctrine; and the kinds of connections made by Baudelaire, Rimbaud, Mallarmé, and Verlaine are of particular significance to Confessional poetry.

The inner world of the Symbolists is at least partially located in the unconscious; dream and illusion, fantasy and imagination are not peripheral but central to their vision. It is a step beyond Donne, since the subjective not only triumphs over the objective, it threatens to annihilate it. In "Le Bateau ivre," turning inward for landscape, Rimbaud has begun the modern displacement of the ego, since the unconscious participates in filling, if not shaping, the poem. In it, Surrealism already has tangible presence. Finally, the quality of imagery dredged up by the Symbolists anticipates Confessional poetry. The ugliness and sordidness of, for example, *Les Fleurs du mal* (1857), which helped earn Symbolism its notoriety, begins to approach taboo. In a dark time, dream manifests itself as nightmare. This is different from earlier nightmare visions, say Dante's *Inferno,* in that it is not placed in the context of some higher vision of order, but rather uneasily seeks its place in the scheme of things, unwilling to be relegated finally to the underworld. But it has not yet, perhaps, found that place.

Surrealism, which has never found many pure disciples in America, but which has left its unmistakable mark on poets as important, and as different, as Wallace Stevens and Hart Crane, sets out to mingle conscious and unconscious perceptions, refusing to recognize the legitimacy of traditional boundaries of the self or the consequent conception of reality those boundaries impose. "There is a hint in all of this," wrote André Breton, "of a belief that there exists a certain spiritual plane on which life and death, the real and the imaginary, the past and the future, the communicable and the incommunicable, the high and the low, are not conceived of as opposites."[3] The world of the Surrealists, then, is the world of the unconscious, for that is preeminently the secular place where all contraries are united, beyond time and before categories of rational thought. However, while it is clear that the premises of Surrealism are crucial to Confessional verse, there are important distinctions to be made.

In Surrealism, the dominance of the unconscious, or at least its uncritical acceptance, is central. Surrealism proposes a new orientation toward reality that in many ways ignores the conscious self. But Confessional poetry attempts something probably more ambitious, more difficult. It does not simply unleash the unconscious, it attempts to incorporate it as a new aspect of consciousness, and so, in a true sense, proposes a redefinition of the self. The Confessionals write from a perspective which has access both to the world of objective experience and to the materials previously repressed. The familiar terms on which the poet and his repressions must remain provoke considerable difficulties, and bring us back to another look at the poetry of madness; for, in the end, it is the Confessional's attitude toward madness that most clearly distinguishes him from the poets in whose traditions he writes.

The notion of the poet as madman goes back at least as far as the divine madness of the Greeks. Homer and Hesiod write of the inspiration of the Muses; no later than the fifth century B.C., the frenzied poet appears, probably a by-product of the Dionysiac movement.[4] Frenzied or not, however, these are instances of possession by the gods; that is to say, the mind of the poet is

3. "Surrealism," in *The Modern Tradition: Backgrounds of Modern Literature,* ed. Richard Ellmann and Charles Feidelson, Jr. (New York: Oxford University Press, 1965), p. 608.

4. See E. R. Dodds, *The Greeks and the Irrational* (Berkeley: University of California Press, 1966), p. 239.

taken over by a more than human agent that presents the gift of a clearer perception of reality. It is the nineteenth century—the Romantic movement again—that introduces the idea of madness as a totally human source of inspiration. The demonic hero of the Romantics, driven mad by his sense of sin, or his refusal to be bound by conventional human limitations, leads to the tormented lives of the Symbolists, to Rimbaud's call for a *déreglement de tous les sens;* and the Surrealists significantly diminish the distance between the voice of the poet and the voice of the madman.

But even in the drug-inspired reveries that became in the early nineteenth century a legitimate source of poetry, all connections with the divine are not totally severed. The idea of inspiration, of access to more than human insight still lingers. And when the sense of the divine is at a minimum, as in the case of the Symbolists, the concept of the poet as sacrificial victim remains, with the implication that the poet has given himself up to some higher power for the greater glory of mankind, or at least of Art. The fact is that through the first half of the twentieth century, madness fell short of becoming both the means and the subject matter of poetry. And not before that group of poets uncomfortably labeled Confessional does madness become not only secularized but, at least in part, deromanticized.

"What's madness but nobility of soul/ At odds with circumstance?"[5] asked Theodore Roethke, who, romantically, liked to see himself as part of that company of mad poets we have just been discussing. But in his poetry, and in the poetry of Lowell, Plath, Sexton, Berryman, and Ginsberg, we discover, maybe for the first time, madness devoid of nobility. In extreme emotional states we find not prophecy, not elevating truths, but the mean, the petty, the embarrassing. In fact, the best evidence supporting the distinguishability of Confessional poetry from its antecedents is the fact that it requires a new theory of the poetry of

5. "In a Dark Time," *The Collected Poems of Theodore Roethke* (New York: Doubleday, 1966), p. 239.

madness to justify its insights. And that justification must be based not on the quasi-mystical intervention of the divine, but rather on the notion that psychotics are suffering from the truth.

In *Love's Body*, Norman Brown suggests precisely this possibility; much of the work of R. D. Laing supports its validity in many specific instances.[6] What Brown and Laing have in common is the sense that men repress huge areas of experience that should be available to consciousness. They propose, therefore, a new definition of consciousness. Much of the criticism of Confessional poetry begins with the assumption that its authors are mad, and that their poetry is therefore either an expression of that madness or an attempt to purge it. The poets are seen in the act of ridding their psyches of garbage, confessing the ugliness within in order to be cleansed. In unsympathetic readings, they emerge as simply self-piteous. However, as we shall see, this approach frequently does not conform to what is happening in the poetry itself, and language is forced into the service of the critic's favorite theory of psychology. Particularly hurtful is the insistence on reading as autobiography poetry that can be said to be that only in a special sense of the word. I would like to suggest instead that these poets are involved in something far more radical than simply daring to speak of things that hitherto have been considered taboo, that they are, in fact, unself-consciously attempting a redefinition of the self of the sort envisioned by Brown and Laing.

A precise formulation of this redefinition must await closer study of particular poets. But even a vague familiarity with their work suggests some generalizations. "I am less impressed than I used to be," writes John Berryman, "by the universal notion of a continuity of personality,"[7] and he proceeds to illustrate this in his "Homage to Anne Bradstreet" and the *Dream Songs*. Rob-

6. See Norman O. Brown, *Love's Body* (New York: Random House, 1968), p. 159, and R. D. Laing, *The Politics of Experience* (New York: Ballantine, 1967), especially ch. 5, "The Schizophrenic Experience," pp. 100–30.

7. Changes," in *Poets on Poetry*, ed. Howard Nemerov (New York: Basic Books, 1966), p. 94.

ert Lowell, obsessed with his country's history as well as his own, breaks down conventional distinctions between public and private experience. Theodore Roethke incorporates into his perceptions of reality a sense of identity between the operations of his unconscious and those of the outer, natural world. Anne Sexton can deal with the events of her life only by recognizing the legitimacy of fantasy, even madness, as commentaries on experience. And Sylvia Plath admits the power of the drive toward destruction, and takes the responsibility for it.

In fact, many of these themes and obsessions are interchangeable among Confessional poets, and the attributions above are arbitrary. But that is precisely why they help define the Confessional's sense of consciousness. The Confessional self cannot easily be pinned down. The normally limited range of personality traits gives way to a broad spectrum of possibilities; and although there is a certain degree of continuity, this self participates in a world of flux from which it can no longer comfortably separate itself. The lack of a narrow, unbending notion of personality results in the erosion of ordinarily clear-cut distinctions between the self and others; on the lower frequencies, to which the Confessionals are most sensitively tuned, similarities among men may be more significant than differences. Nor can valid distinctions between inner and outer lives be drawn. From a conventional point of view, the Confessional self must appear nearly psychotic, or, at best, flirting with a dangerously dark, dangerously unorganized encounter with experience. Consequently, the relationship between the psychological state of the poet and his poetry has been a major concern of critics of Confessional verse. Sylvia Plath, John Berryman, and Anne Sexton did commit suicide. Theodore Roethke and Robert Lowell spent a good deal of time in mental institutions. The obvious question is whether or not the decision to expand the boundaries of the self involves the risk of sanity, if not the risk of life itself.

A. Alvarez, who had himself attempted suicide, makes the most explicit connection between the life and art of Sylvia Plath: "The achievement of her final style is to make poetry and

death inseparable. The one could not exist without the other.
. . . Poetry of this order is a murderous art." In a reprinting of
the essay in which these remarks were originally made, Alvarez
denies that he had suggested that madness or suicidal tendencies would necessarily result in good poetry, or that they were
inevitably produced by the writing of poetry that touches the extremes.

> But I did mean to imply that this kind of writing involves an element
> of risk. The Extremist artist sets out deliberately to explore the roots
> of his emotions, the obscurist springs of his personality, maybe even
> the sickness he feels himself prey to, "giving himself over to it," as I
> have written elsewhere, "for the sake of the range and intensity of
> his art."[8]

M. L. Rosenthal reaches similar conclusions, at least in so far as
Sylvia Plath is concerned. "She chose, if that is the word, what
seems to me the one alternative position to Lowell's along the
dangerous confessional way, that of literally committing her
own predicaments in the interests of her art until the one was
so involved with the other that no return was possible."[9]

The assumption implicit in both analyses is that the Confessional poet, or at least a certain kind of Confessional poet, risks
destruction by incorporating as part of conscious experience attitudes, fantasies, and perceptions that the rest of us prudently
leave buried in dark, unexplored corners of the mind. This
seems to form an indirect challenge to Brown and Laing, who
vouch for the value of making conscious much of that which
has been previously repressed.

Considering the nature of the lives led by the most prominent
Confessional poets, the hypothesis that the writing of this kind
of poetry may produce the side effect of madness or death
seems reasonable. But if this conclusion is possible, it is not
necessary. True, the Confessionals explored dark corners of the
mind and used what they found there to write their poems.
True, their own lives were tormented as a consequence of their
psychic disturbances. But is is just as reasonable to suppose

8. "Sylvia Plath," p. 73.   9. *The New Poets*, p. 83.

that rather than choosing to be overwhelmed in order to write poetry, they chose to write poetry in order to avoid being overwhelmed. And it is just as possible that the dealing with charged materials was in the interest of health, an effort that fell short rather than one that was misdirected.

There is no real chance of resolving the question. But this much, at least, is true. It is not the pathology of the Confessional poets that we respond to, except in so far as we can recognize that "pathology" as part of our own psychological make-up. Or, to put it another way, the Confessionals transform that which is pathological in their own lives into that which is existential. And whether or not the act of writing this poetry is destructive or healing in nature, the poem itself proposes a new model of the self, not as a distortion, but rather as a more complete, a more honest, confrontation with reality. This, however, is a proposition that must be demonstrated by the poetry itself. And the poetry that I have selected as representative of Confessional verse is that of Robert Lowell, Sylvia Plath, and John Berryman.

Robert Lowell's *Life Studies* is an attempt to reveal a personality—or rather a persona—in all its complexity. What is truly unique in this particular endeavor, however, is not to be found in any specific poem but in the construction of the book as a whole. Part One contains four poems, all in some way related to what might be termed western history. Part Two is the prose memoir of Lowell's childhood. Part Three consists of four poems, each devoted to a writer or philosopher. Part Four is divided into two sections, the first a series of poems about Lowell's family, ending with his own stay in a mental institution, the second, five poems presenting a complex view of Lowell's psyche in the present. That all these poems belong in the same volume, with perhaps more claim to unity than many other collections of verse, has never been questioned. But most critics have assumed that a searing poem like "Skunk Hour" is more properly "Confessional" than a more public poem like "Inauguration Day: January 1953." In a sense, of course, it is. However, the uniqueness of Lowell's volume lies precisely in the fact that all the poems are necessary parts of the portrait of Lowell, not simply because they provide necessary background, but because they are all essential perceptions of the persona, all equally "Confessional"; or rather, there is no Confessional act unless all perspectives have been utilized.

In fact, the technique of *Life Studies* is far more like that of Ezra Pound's major work than has been generally recognized. "Hugh Selwyn Mauberley," for example, employs multiple perspectives with the same intention of building up a single persona through discrete perceptions rather than attempting definitively to characterize that persona from one point of view. For Lowell experiences real difficulty in trying to define his own identity. Possibly this is a consequence of psychologically based confusions. It may simply be the case that a poet with an especially tenuous sense of self—like Lowell, or Roethke, or, perhaps, any of the Confessionals—may count himself fortunate that he writes in an age obsessed by crises of identity. But it is also possible that Lowell rejects a simplistic view of the self, that rather than understanding it to be a relatively constant core, of which relationships with the outer world are important manifestations, he conceives of the self as inseparable from those relationships and therefore impossible to isolate as a discrete entity.

Robert Lowell, in that case, must be understood not simply in terms of the agonizing explorations of his madness and his relationship with his family and his wife. His meditations on history, his imaginative re-creations of the minds of other writers, even his own fantasies, are important precisely because they are not direct descriptions and analyses of personal experience, and therefore, especially when juxtaposed to appropriate fragments of his own life, may be especially revealing. The job of the critic then becomes similar to the job of the psychoanalyst, who listens not to his patients' explanations of the course of their daily lives, but rather to the bare juxtaposition of events, fantasies, commentaries, in order to perceive the truth beyond the intellectualizations of consciousness. The book of poems in itself becomes, in a sense with which William Carlos Williams would have been quite comfortable, a complex, imaginative construct which stands juxtaposed to Lowell's own experience as well as our own. For Lowell, as he made clear shortly after the publication of *Life Studies,* was perfectly aware that he had created a version of himself, rather than a definitive representation.

> There's a good deal of tinkering with fact. You leave out a lot, and emphasize this and not that. Your actual experience is a complete flux. I've invented facts and changed things, and the whole balance of the poem was something invented. . . . And so there was always that standard of truth which you wouldn't ordinarily have in poetry—the reader was to believe he was getting the *real* Robert Lowell.[10]

Part of what Lowell tells us, perhaps the major part, is not peculiar to Confessional poetry. The notion that poets lie in order to say the truth is familiar; so is the idea that a condensed version of a complex reality requires selection and distortion of materials. But Lowell goes beyond that. "Your actual experience is a complete flux." The implication is not only that the literal truth is not necessarily essential truth, but that the very existence of literal truth in the ordinary sense is in doubt. The literal truth about the self depends on the ability to locate that self unambiguously in time and space. A particular moment must be separated from surrounding moments, the individual must be separated from the world he experiences. When the poet loses confidence in his ability to do precisely that, he must find alternate means of communicating his sense of experience. For to suggest that a traditional conception of reality is no longer valid is not to insist that there is no longer a real world.

In this light, the structure of *Life Studies* has added significance. The first section, the meditations on history, tells us about Lowell in an obvious way, since he re-creates or comments upon historical events, and thus reveals his own interpretations of the public world. However, the poems have even more

10. *Writers at Work: The Paris Review Interviews,* Second Series (New York: Viking, 1963), p. 349.

significance: that public world becomes part of Lowell's *private* experience. In "Inauguration Day: January 1953," for example, Lowell's characterization of Eisenhower as the "Cyclonic zero of the word"[11] is surely a straight-forward political and cultural commentary, and in that sense tells us something about the author. But if we compare the imagery of the poem—zero, ice, wheels that no longer move—to that of a more obviously personal poem, like "Memories of West Street and Lepke," with its metaphors of tranquilization, prison, the electric chair, and its almost explicit drawing of connections between the condition of society and the condition of the poet, we find that Lowell is looking not simply at Eisenhower and the nation, he is looking very closely at himself as well. The wheels that no longer move are, of course, the Republic's, but they are also Robert Lowell's. And that "Cyclonic zero" is, after all, of the word, an appropriate commentary on a poet doubting his own commitments.

The dangers implicit in this methodology—some of them at least—are obvious. If everything that one perceives can be reduced to a projection of oneself, the resulting vision must be solipsistic. But this judgment depends upon the validity of distinctions drawn between the self and the other. In a sense, not only is solipsism not the inevitable outcome of Lowell's stance, it is effectively eliminated as a possibility. For although the knowledge of his poetry is subjective, this is a subjectivity that unifies rather than divides.

Actually, what Lowell is doing should be relatively familiar. He establishes a metaphor: as Ike is to the Republic, so this period of "tranquilization" is to Lowell. The difficulty is that half the metaphor is unstated, and would not, in fact, be detectable without the illuminating context of *Life Studies* as a whole. Even this is recognizable. Is it not precisely the methodology of the Symbolists; for that matter, is not a symbol simply half a metaphor cut loose from its other half? But while it is useful to notice the extent to which Lowell operates within the Symbolist

11. *Life Studies* (Vintage: New York 1959), p. 7. Page references will hereafter be given parenthetically in the text.

tradition, it is also necessary to understand the ways in which he alters that tradition. For if the Symbolist seems to postulate a ground of meaning outside the ordinary scope of the individual, Lowell seems to postulate one inside. The world of spirit for Lowell is a psychological reality. And what makes all the difference in the world is the fact that Lowell seems to take literally the connections between inner and outer realities. That is, not only is the poet free to describe an inner truth in terms of a totally unrelated outer event, such as Lowell's own spiritual impasse by Eisenhower's inauguration, there is in addition some unstated principle of synchronicity, a real, if acausal, link between the two areas of experience. That this principle is operating in Lowell's poetry is rather difficult to demonstrate. I will be content to point out that Lowell makes use of correspondences between inner and outer worlds so consistently that he seems to count on the availability of those connections; and whether or not that availability is a consequence of synchronicity, it is the cornerstone of Lowell's poetry.

"A Mad Negro Soldier Confined at Munich," for example, similarly presents a situation that not only relates to Lowell's own experience of reality, but also seems intimately connected to it. Like Lowell in "Memories of West Street and Lepke," the Negro soldier is imprisoned. Like Lowell in "Walking in the Blue," he is in an insane asylum. As in "To Speak of Woe that Is in Marriage," sexual impulses are violent, desperate attempts to hold on to a disappearing self. As in "Man and Wife," woman is not only the recipient of that "trolley-pole sparking" (p. 8) violence, but also mother and comforter. In fact, there is ample evidence for thinking of the mad Negro soldier as a persona for Lowell. As I have already suggested, there are great similarities between the methodology of *Life Studies* and that of Pound's "Mauberley." As in "Mauberley" the principal character in the poem is developed not simply through direct treatment but also through the personae of Dante Gabriel Rossetti, M. Verog, Brennbaum, the Stylist, and pictures of the society Mauberley inhabits, so Robert Lowell's own character is at least partially developed by a similar use of masks—the mad Negro Soldier and Eisenhower as well as the more obvious Ford, Santayana, Schwartz, and Crane of Part Three. Of course, "Mauberley" himself may be a mask, albeit a self-consciously ironic one, for Pound himself. And here too the comparison holds, for we have already seen that the Lowell of *Life Studies* might well be thought of as a mask constructed to present the reader with a "real" Robert Lowell, though there is reason to doubt whether such a thing, in the sense that reader would intend, really exists.

The other poems of the opening section may similarly be read as manifestations of Lowell's inner life—although it would be well to state here the caution implicit throughout this discussion, that my intention is to expand more conventional readings of the poems, not replace them. "Beyond the Alps," then, receives added dimension as a statement of Lowell's own spiritual emptiness, his own failure to climb Everest, to "understand" the world of the spirit. "The Banker's Daughter" enters that shadowy area of relations between men and women where the woman's relation to husband and son, and her roles as protectress and victim, become confused. It is an area of experience to which Lowell will return in "Man and Wife."

The place of the prose memoir "91 Revere Street" in *Life Studies* has always been relatively clear. The glimpse of Lowell's childhood becomes a basis upon which many subsequent poems seem to depend, or at least by means of which their significance to the reader may be enriched. His father's apparent weakness, his mother's intrusive power, are dominant motifs. And Lowell's relationship with women is given an extra twist by his attendance at a school in which the upper grades were for girls only: "To be a boy at Brimmer was to be small, denied, weak" (p. 25).

The slight modification I would propose is that "91 Revere Street" be considered not a fragment of autobiographical prose inserted in a book of poetry, but rather an integral part of the single poem that *Life Studies* is, in the same manner that prose excerpts become part of Pound's *Cantos* and Williams' *Paterson*. Rather than a repository of factual background, a secondary service to the poems on the one hand, a limit to their possible interpretations on the other, "91 Revere Street" should be seen as an additional perspective, an independent point of view which may explain, support, or even contradict any other part of the poem. This distinction may not cause any drastic changes in interpretation, but I intend it as a corrective to too neat an understanding of interlocking parts, all of which obligingly conform to one another. In fact, "91 Revere Street" itself is representative of that neatness. It accepts the continuity of narrative time, the consistency of a single point of view. Continually interjecting his opinions and interpretations, Lowell further asserts the capacity of the individual rationally to organize his experience. "91 Revere Street," then, stands out from the rest of *Life Studies* not simply because it is prose, but also because it is a champion of the coherence that the book as a whole recognizes is not available to it.

Ford Madox Ford as a great artist, insufficiently recognized by the murderous society in which he lived; George Santayana, the Catholic who died "unbelieving, unconfessed and unreceived" (p. 49); Delmore Schwartz, whose paranoia translated itself into universal *Angst;* and Hart Crane, far more Confessional in the words given him by Lowell than in his own poetry, in fact, here, the quintessential Confessional poet, requiring significant emotional investment from his audience. These are the occupants of Part Three of *Life Studies*.

Like everything else in *Life Studies,* each of the four poems can stand on its own. However, each also forms part of the mosaic that will finally give us a real Robert Lowell. Just as in a dream each dream-person embodies, among other things, those aspects of ourselves with which we identify the prototype of the dream-person, so Ford, Santayana, Schwartz, and Crane *are* aspects of Robert Lowell.

We have already seen that this is the methodology of Ezra Pound. But at this point, a distinction should be drawn between the approaches of Pound and those of Lowell. Pound is, for better or worse, a poet of surfaces. In psychological terms, it seems fair to say that he deals with behavior rather than motives. Lowell, however, while he rejects conventional notions of unity, operates at various depths in creating his own mosaic. Lowell does examine indirect evidence as a way of defining Robert Lowell, but he also deals with direct introspection. He is not naive as to motive; that is, he does not suppose that motives for human actions can always be easily distinguished in order to determine the correct one. But if Pound obliterates individuality by subsuming everything within the bounds of his psyche, by fashioning, in Joycean terms, an individual who embodies a culture, Lowell remembers always the tension between the individual and his world; although boundaries cannot be defined, and are, in fact, in constant flux, the self persists, uncertain, maybe, of what it is. Because of this, Lowell's poetic voice is more nearly constant than Pound's, and his moral concerns focus on individual responsibility rather than ideology.

Part Four of *Life Studies* is in some ways representative of Lowell's attitude toward the "self" in its complexity. On the one hand, by dealing with grandparents, uncles, parents, and only finally with himself, he places himself on a temporal continuum; the implication is that he cannot be understood except as part of his family. On the other hand, the sequence leads inexorably to the poet himself, and, whatever the merits of the individual poems, their inclusion can only be justified by their relation to the poet's own experience. In fact, one might almost say that in the writing of this section, and of *Life Studies* as a whole, Lowell proves that his self exists, since it is there to provide focus to a series of poems.

The most convenient way to understand the precise function of the family poems of Part Four is to see how they compare with the "91 Revere Street" section in their treatment of a particular figure in the poet's life, his father. While not entirely unsympathetic to his father in the prose section, Lowell essentially perceives him the way his mother does, the way she wants her son to perceive him. His father describes his resignation from the Navy "with an unnatural and importunate jocularity" (p. 40). He "pitifully" bemoans his inability to replace Navy friends. Near the end of the passage, Commander Billy abhors "Mother's dominion over my father" (p. 44).

The poems devoted to Lowell's father in Part Four are clearly about the same defeated man. In "Commander Lowell," we learn how the father, as a Naval officer not "serious" enough for his wife's socialite crowd, leaves his job in the Navy for Lever Brothers, and, to complete the thorough-going humiliation, deeds his wife his property. But Lowell does not leave it at that. He pushes backwards, so that we see his father in more dignified circumstances:

> *Smiling on all,*
> *Father was once successful enough to be lost*
> *in the mob of ruling-class Bostonians.*
> *As early as* 1928,
> *he owned a house converted to oil,*
> *and redecorated by the architect*
> *of St. Mark's School. . . . Its main effect*
> *was a drawing room, "longitudinal as Versailles,"*
> *its ceiling, roughened with oatmeal, was blue as the sea.*
> *And once*
> *nineteen, the youngest ensign in his class,*
> *he was "the old man" of a gunboat on the Yangtze.*   (p. 66)

Like an elevator falling in its shaft, Lowell plummets suddenly into the past, racing past the years of castration to a time when the Commander had his place in a social world, to the time earlier still when he owned a house that evokes thoughts of Versailles—another relic of a dead age—and finally, to his precocious naval career. It is, first, a qualified rehabilitation of Commander Lowell's reputation, at least restoring to him the effectual days of his youth, if it cannot create for him the dignity of his later years. And this, of course, represents at least the partial restoration of a strong masculine figure to incorporate into Robert Lowell's own experience, even though this image remains vulnerable to the assault of a strong woman, which, later poems strongly suggest, is precisely the reality with which Lowell must deal. So that the problem of the book, and of his life, is to recapture his father's youth and to avoid the perils of his maturity. But it is only when we reach "Memories of West Street and Lepke" in Part Five, with its evocation of Lowell's more effectual youth and his present tranquilization, that we fully understand that, like everything else in the book, this poem is about Lowell's own experience. In recognizing that his father too had a fiery youth, only to slip into passive age, Lowell casts doubt on his own future. He must struggle to keep, or to regain, what he had. Finally, the past in general is revealed as a possible source of unexpected vitality, so that *Life Studies* can be seen as therapy as well as art.

"Terminal Days at Beverly Farms" should be one of the most terrifying poems in the book. And yet this account of the death of Lowell's father is strangely comforting. His father's "newly dieted figure was vitally trim" (p. 67). Each morning he steals off to the Maritime Museum at Salem, where he calls the curator "the commander of the Swiss Navy." In imagination, the father has returned to the days of his strength. Lowell selects a physical characteristic ironically inappropriate to his father's impending death: "His vision was still twenty-twenty." In this context, the poem's—and the father's—last words, are ambiguous. "I feel awful," he says. This understatement, coming after a morning of anxious smiling, can be seen either as the final expression of his passivity, or as calm acceptance of the inevitable.

"Father's Bedroom" reinforces the complex network of associations running through the sequence. The book found in the bedroom, which "has had hard usage / on the Yangtze River, China" (p. 69), takes us back to the days of Commander Lowell's strength. However, the inscription, "Robbie from Mother," tells us what use to make of that allusion. Robbie can be either Lowell's father or the poet himself. In this case, ambiguity suggests identification. But like his father, "Mother" remains present, a powerful figure; "Mother's bed," which will appear in "Man and Wife," is an effective foil to "Father's Bedroom."

Nonetheless, in "For Sale," Lowell's insight once again belies the one-sided interpretation of the relationship between father and mother to emerge from "91 Revere Street." The house is now for sale. But the poem's most powerful image is of neither house nor father.

> *Ready, afraid*
> *of living alone till eighty,*
> *Mother mooned in a window,*
> *as if she had stayed on a train*
> *one stop past her destination.*   (p. 70)

Lowell suggests that strength or weakness, as we have understood them so far, are superficial characteristics. Beneath the surface is the real relationship, a web of interdependences that transcend hierarchy. Without the weak, passive father, the mother's own strength disappears.

It is not that "91 Revere Street" was wrong. That was one way of putting it, maybe as accurate as any. And the book is not an attempt to represent a family saga; it is given life by Robert Lowell's re-enactment of his own experience. While we are always able to say—theoretically—that the poem is a projection of its author's psyche at the time of writing, such considerations remain theory except in specialized studies. But by constructing his book as he does, Lowell forces the reader to take into account this dimension of the poetry. By shifting point of view, and including materials that are subtly contradictory, Lowell fragments experience into a series of intersecting planes rather than a sequential narrative. By linking apparently disparate areas of experience through imagery and action, he undermines the notion of distinct personality. In short, the world observed and the observer of that world can not be decisively separated. So that what would ordinarily be considered context, becomes foreground, a vital manifestation of the poet's psychic reality. In fact, we may be reminded that without a fixed point of view, there is nothing but foreground.

Toward the end of the first section of Part Four, Robert Lowell—the adult Robert Lowell—becomes the explicit subject of his poetry for the first time. In "Walking in the Blue" and "Home After Three Months Away," the dizzying plunges into the past of the poems dealing with Lowell's father are now metamorphized into the sense that the poet's own life may be proceeding backwards. Is there a relationship between the home for the mentally ill and Beverly Farms, the site of Commander Lowell's death? Is one of the several reasons for Lowell's preoccupation with his children the fact that he himself is now the father, and therefore fully liable to the things that happen to fathers? Where incident fails to establish links among the poems, language or image does. The "turtle-necked French sailor's jersey" of "Walking in the Blue" associates Lowell with the navy, and therefore with his father. The last line of "Home After Three Months Away"—"Cured, I am frizzled, stale and small"—takes the poet back to his own childhood, to his father's final years, but also establishes connections between Lowell and the mad Negro soldier and his electric shock, and Czar Lepke and his electric chair (pp. 76, 78). And the conclusion of "Walking in the Blue" has its own reverberations. The metal shaving mirrors—metal so they cannot be shattered and the pieces used as suicidal or homicidal weapons—distort reality, and in that sense become images of the poet's "objective" reality. But the poet will not be cheated totally of his violence:

We are all old-timers,
each of us holds a locked razor.

The razor is Lowell's own violence. But just as his father's world has become enmeshed with his own, so his world becomes part of his father's. The "old-timer" reminds us of Commander Lowell and makes us aware of the locked razor that passive, overwhelmed man had for so many years carried within him.

Section II of Part Four brings *Life Studies* to its carefully prepared climax. "Memories of West Street and Lepke" in particular gathers up strands (p. 79). Living on "Boston's / 'hardly passionate Marlborough Street,' " Lowell first appears in terms we have to this point associated with his father. In this part of the city, even the man scavenging in trash cans is a "young Republican," recalling "Inauguration Day: January 1953."

"These are the tranquilized *Fifties*," Lowell announces, "and I am forty." This is the dominant image of *Life Studies:* the tranquilized man, the tranquilized country, both with a more energetic past, both needing to be shocked into renewed vitality.

Lowell recalls his days as "a fire-breathing Catholic C. O.," making his "manic statement"—that is, his refusal to participate in World War II—and, like the Negro soldier in Munich, incarcerated for his actions. The ironies of that earlier poem, the fact that it is set in Munich, the fact that the jailers are American soldiers, the fact that the Negro is, like the Jews in Germany, part of a persecuted group, are emphasized by the imprisonment of a man who refused to fight, who is perceived as part of a minority, by those who are waging the war. The presence of the Negro boy helps recall the earlier poem for the reader who has trouble making these connections.

In a book preoccupied with violence—with violence expressed and violence repressed—it seems natural that Lowell would create a hierarchy of violence in the prison. At one extreme is Abramowitz, a vegetarian even more pacifistic than Lowell; there is the Negro boy, imprisoned, maybe, for being a victim; the Hollywood pimps, Bioff and Brown, who eventually beat up Abramowitz; and finally, Czar Lepke, of Murder Incorporated, whose American flags and ribbon of Easter palm reveal his underlying association with prevailing political and religious establishments.

However, although we are clearly meant to perceive the additional irony of murderer and conscientious objector sharing the same prison, Lepke is not viewed unsympathetically; or at least Lowell does not choose to see himself as totally apart from, and superior to, Lepke.

> *Flabby, bald, lobotomized,*
> *he drifted in a sheepish calm,*
> *where no agonizing reappraisal*
> *jarred his concentration on the electric chair—*
> *hanging like an oasis in his air*
> *of lost connections. . . .*

Lobotomized, Lepke's condition is not totally unrelated to Lowell's present state of tranquilization. And like Lepke, Lowell is experiencing a sense of "lost connections." The full range of human possibilities represented in the poem become Lowell's own possibilities, and it is precisely because of this that they are included in the poem. For while the chief distinction between Lepke and Lowell is that the former is a murderer, the latter a pacifist, we now become aware of a secondary distinction which may, in fact, be more nearly fundamental: Lowell *is* jarred by an agonizing reappraisal, that is, the sorting of possibilities, the comparisons between past and present, that constitute the poem.

"Tamed by *Miltown,* we lie on Mother's bed": this is the opening line of "Man and Wife" (p. 81). Lowell picks up and further elaborates the theme of tranquilization, whose dominance becomes more and more evident, as does the latent violence this tranquilization is intended to cover up. And there is no more appropriate place to experience both sides of what we may now understand to be a single theme than Mother's bed. For we are shown a Lowell who has at the same time taken his father's place, and therefore become his father, and a Lowell who is still—like his father—a passive child in relation to women.

In a reversal of the roles of the traditional Orpheus myth, the poet is for a fourth time led out of the "homicidal" kingdom of the mad by his wife. A flashback shows the poet drunk—alchohol here suggests the child at his bottle, dependent and helpless—at the feet of his more than competent future wife. As a matter of fact, her intense involvement in political issues compares favorably to Lowell's own tranquilization, which the book has revealed as a political as well as psychological fact. So that, in a sense, his wife represents a part of his own past. But she also is a link to his more distant past, to his childhood.

Sleepless, you hold
your pillow to your hollows like a child;
your old-fashioned tirade–

loving, rapid, merciless—
breaks like the Atlantic Ocean on my head.

There is an ambiguity here. Is it the pillow that is like a child being held by his wife; or is his wife like a child holding a pillow? And this ambiguity is reflected in the loving, merciless tirade. His wife is both awesome and diminutive, both overwhelming and of human dimensions. Lowell himself, already revealed as Ford Madox Ford, George Santayana, Delmore Schwartz, and Hart Crane, rolled up in one, with a locked razor inside to boot, is sufficiently complex. He is the child, he is the homicidal madman.

And in " 'To Speak of Woe that Is in Marriage,' " the alternative side of the poet is revealed. Instead of the tranquilized child, we find, as seen from the wife's point of view, a manic husband: "This screwball might kill his wife, then take the pledge" (p. 82). The locked razor is opened—indeed, the poem's "razor's edge" recalls that image—the violence of the Negro soldier merges with Lowell's own fierce anger. At this stage of *Life Studies,* each new poem sets into motion reverberations that dance through the earlier poems of the book, weaving them together as part of the texture of Lowell's psyche.

In "Skunk Hour," which finds the poet searching out "lovecars" on lover's lane, Lowell articulates the terror that has lurked behind most of the volume: "My mind's not right" (p. 84). Later, echoing Marlowe's Mephistopholes, he says, "I myself am hell; / nobody's here—" Although it is probably not precisely what Lowell had in mind when he wrote them, those lines remind us of the main thrust of this study. "Nobody" is there; the self has lost control, has abandoned its role of arbiter of experience to the extent that that center of consciousness seems no longer to exist. The considerable terror of the poem is abated if not resolved by the mother skunk swilling the garbage pails; she "will not scare." It is difficult to know how to take these lines. With her "ostrich tail," there is some suggestion that the mother skunk perseveres only by ignoring aspects of reality that will not disappear. In addition, she is not only a member of a species with an unsavory reputation, she is also still another version of the mother, strong to be sure, but hardly a source of comfort for such as Lowell. Nonetheless, her animal, prerational courage is perhaps what is left to us; and in rooting among garbage cans, she is an image not of the mother but of Lowell himself. Like the poet, she has endured.

Earliest editions of *Life Studies* did not contain "Colonel Shaw and the Massachusetts' 54th," which now stands last in the volume. Later renamed "For the Union Dead," it became the cornerstone of that more public collection of poems, to which it gave its name. For us, it represents a convenient introduction to that point of intersection between public and private worlds that has increasingly become the domain of Robert Lowell's poetry.

Lowell begins by contemplating the abandoned wreck of the old South Boston Aquarium, and, longing "for the dark downward and vegetating kingdom / of the fish and reptile" (p. 85), he recalls steamshovels like yellow dinosaurs preparing the way for the garage at Boston Common. This in turn takes his gaze to the statue of Colonel Shaw and his Negro regiment, which "sticks like a fishbone / in the City's throat." Toward the end of the poem, Lowell makes use of techniques much more commonly associated with Pound and Williams.

> *The ditch is nearer.*
> *There are no statues for the last war here;*
> *on Boylston Street, a commercial photograph*
> *shows Hiroshima boiling*
>
> *over a Mosler Safe, the "Rock of Ages"*
> *that survived the blast. Space is nearer.*
> *When I crouch to my television set,*
> *the drained faces of Negro children rise like balloons.*

As bad as the hypocrisy evoked by the Civil War memorial may be, it can hardly match that "monument" to World War II, the advertisement in which the Mosler Safe Company exploits the devastation of the Atomic Bomb in order to sell its products; for Lowell, whose Conscientious Objector status during the war was publicly linked by him with the allied bombings of civilian centers, the irony must be especially bitter. By juxtaposition, Lowell connects the dropping of that bomb with "the drained faces of Negro children." The technique is here eloquent, perhaps more eloquent than a Pound or Williams would have permitted. It reminds us that the Bomb was dropped on people who were not white, that we are a commercial society that will profit from any disaster, be it the dropping of the Bomb or the destruction by slower and subtler methods of a significant portion of our own society, that we in many ways have become indistinguishable from the "immoral" enemies from whom we have saved the world.

Finally, we return to the Aquarium, and as the "giant finned cars nose forward like fish," now that a garage has replaced the Aquarium, we perceive ourselves as part of some primitively savage world. In a way, this vision brings to an end the period of tranquilization and marks a renewed concern with the realities of a political and public universe, as opposed to the self-absorption of recent years. But in other ways, this poem is not so much a repudiation of those concerns as a new way to experience them.

"The cowed, compliant fish," for example, which Lowell used to watch at the Aquarium, recall the "minnows, slaves of habit," who swim in "their air-conditioned bowl" in "A Mad Negro Soldier Confined at Munich" (p. 8). The Civil War monument brings to mind the comparisons between Eisenhower and Grant in "Inauguration Day: January 1953." And, as "a fishbone / in the City's throat," it becomes a kind of locked razor. In any case, it is precisely the lack of responsiveness to social and political reality that Lowell attributes to the City that has been his own complaint, diagnosed and maybe in part cured in *Life Studies*. For having explored some of the less glamorous corners of Lowell's childhood world, we can no longer think of the "fishbone" as purely external in origin; it is the product of personal anger and frustration as well. In demonstrating the connection between public and private concerns, Lowell is hardly breaking new ground. But when he is willing to make that abstraction concrete by opening up areas of the private that are usually kept closed, and when he pushes to extremes the possibilities of dealing with one area of experience not directly but in terms of the other, he has at least some claim to have opened up new poetic territory.

If *Life Studies* is the quintessential Confessional volume of poetry in that it explores those areas of experience previously taboo in close detail, *Notebook 1967–68,* in its various incarnations, represents the logical extension of an equally essential aspect of Confessional verse, its merging of public and private worlds. However, we should preface our discussion by noticing again that there is much about this book to place it in the company of works by Pound, Williams, and Olson. First, it seems to be one of those poems that is very difficult to finish. After its original publication in 1969, it reappeared as *Notebook,* revised and expanded, in 1970. In 1973, it had not only again been revised and expanded, it had now split, amoeba-like, into two books, *History* and *For Lizzie and Harriet.* Presumably it is now locked into its final form, although it would not be a total surprise were Lowell to decide to have at it again. What is perhaps more interesting is that in order to pin the poem down, Lowell found it necessary to separate the more obviously public and more obviously private sections of the poem. We may surmise, then, that it is precisely that mixture that places the poem in the company of works whose shape must be discovered in the process of creation rather than predetermined, and which form open rather than closed systems. Second, the work plays with traditional form, treating the sonnet in much the same fashion as Pound treated the canto, recalling the sonnet sequence as Pound recalled the *Commedia;* each writer shows himself as attracted to form, so that we are all the more convinced when conventional form is rejected. And finally, even with its chronological organization, the book operates by means of juxtapositions rather than sequence, and produces a sense of fragmentation rather than conventional unity. It is all the more telling, then, that Lowell insists on treating the book as one poem: "the poems in this book are written as one poem, jagged in pattern,

but not a conglomeration or sequence of related material."[12]
This is not a notion of a poem that could have been understood
before Pound's *Cantos*.

In that same "Afterthought" in which he describes *Notebook
1967–68* as a single poem, Lowell makes another interesting
remark about his poetic techniques. "I lean heavily to the rational, but am devoted to surrealism." In 1970, he changed the
name of the object of his devotion to "unrealism."[13] Why Lowell
rejects the traditional term for the use of language that is logically contradictory, based on fantasy and dream as well as "real"
life is not immediately evident. However, aside from the fact
that he may simply find his newer term more accurate and less
French, Lowell may also wish to distinguish his own work, in
intent if not in method, from that of poets more involved in the
pyrotechnics of language than in the creation of convincing fic-
tions of the self. Perhaps most important, the new term has
none of the ambiguities of surrealism and represents a full commitment to that world that seems objectively insubstantial, but
which we have already learned to associate with revised definitions of experience, with a new conception of the self.

One of the best roads of access to *Notebook 1967–68*—we will
begin our discussion with the original version, so as to understand better the significance of later revisions—is through the
sequence "April 8, 1968." In the first poem of that sequence,
"Two Walls," Lowell writes of the confrontation of two white
walls, alludes to the pursuit of Don Giovanni, and then, somewhat mysteriously it may seem, plunges into extreme, generalized despair.

> *At this point of civilization, this point of the world,*
> *the only satisfactory companion we*
> *can imagine is death—this morning, skin lumping in my*
>   *throat,*
> *I lie here, heavily breathing, the soul of New York.*[14]

12. *Notebook 1967–68* (New York: Farrar, Straus and Giroux, 1969), p. 159.
13. *Notebook* (New York: Farrar, Straus and Giroux, 1970), p. 262.
14. *Notebook 1967–68*, p. 87.

It is a personal image; the poet's pain is physical experience. The subject is somewhat obscured until we consult the list of dates provided by the poet at the volume's conclusion. Martin Luther King was murdered on April 4, 1968. That is surely what the poem is about in the sense that it pinpoints the source of Lowell's despondency. But while it is hardly earthshaking for a writer to claim to have been upset by King's assassination, it is something else to make that pain so intimate, so that it becomes difficult to think of the public event as existing in an outer world. Lowell seems somehow to have incorporated that world into his own nervous system. The "subject" of the poem is, in fact, so thoroughly swallowed that not only is he not mentioned by name, the fact that there *is* a distinct subject is anything but clear. The poem is testimony to experience only; that is the only "reality" it recognizes.

In the case of that year's second assassination, Robert Kennedy's, Lowell names the event in the title of the short sequence memorializing it. But the mixture of public and private is still very much in effect. The moment of the poem is the "first ride of the summer" with his daughter, Harriet. The poem becomes the poet's response to his daughter's response: "I trapped in words, / you gagging your head-over-heels articulation" (p. 118). The public only has meaning when it is experienced in terms of the private; better still, the distinction between inner and outer no longer holds. How could we ever have thought to respond to an objective event without regard to the immediate context within which that event is perceived? To effect that kind of abstraction requires the rational center of consciousness that Lowell has, for this volume at least, excluded from his poetry.

It is easy enough to go through the book and multiply examples of public events encased in private experience. But we should take care to ascertain that this is a consequence of Lowell's way of perceiving the world in general and not simply a function of his response to political reality. In the first poem in the sequence "Charles River," Lowell gets to the heart of the matter. We begin with a landscape in motion: sycamore trees casting shadows on the curving stream, a young girl with her

escort walking along the river. The stream seems to display for
Lowell a consistency he himself lacks. His own coursing
blood—symbol of body, animality, all that lies beneath consciousness—performs "its variations, / its endless handspring
around the single I . . ." (p. 36). True, the poem seems also to
be about lovers coming together; but Lowell has chosen to
express this union in terms of fragmentation of the self. And the
poem's last lines add support to that reading.

> *if we leaned forward, and should dip a finger*
> *into this river's momentary black flow,*
> *the infinite small stars would break like fish.*

The stars, reflected in the water, appear as fish. According to
the doctrine of correspondences, as above, so below. But Lowell
takes his correspondences seriously; he fantasizes his ability to
disturb the stars by disturbing the "fish," which in phenome-
nological terms, is perfectly reasonable. At all times, it is the
perceptual field rather than the "reality" beyond that field that
arrests the poet's attention. In addition, in a book so devoted to
an understanding of history, the association between the river
and the temporal stream is unavoidable. It is as if the notion of
significant form in history holds only as long as one does not too
closely examine the flow. What appears to be fish is no more
than illusion. In this poem, at least, there seems to be a touch of
nostalgia for the solider world that Lowell finds so elusive, for
the "single I" that for as long as he can remember has been
swept up in the welter of experience. As Lowell says at the
conclusion of the fifth poem of "Mexico," in lines that might
well stand as an epigraph not only to *Notebook 1967–68* and its
immediate successors, but to his entire work:

> *I am learning to live in history.*
> *What is history? What you cannot touch.* (p. 60)

Rather than multiply examples of this mélange of private and
public, we can quickly arrive at an understanding of what *Notebook 1967–68*, or, for that matter, *Notebook*, is, if we compare

it to its latest version, *History*. The earlier books derive their organization from the creative act itself. Like the *Cantos,* they break down categories of time and space. Poems about Agamemnon, George Grosz, Che Guevara, Sir Thomas More, T. S. Eliot, Cranach, Robert Kennedy, and Milton, to name but a few of the heroes that populate *Notebook,* rub shoulders without any noticeable discomfort, without any need to justify their proximity. As we have already seen, individual poems obliterate distinctions between inner and outer worlds. In addition, poems that are devoted to either one or the other area of experience are juxtaposed as easily as poems devoted to any of the disparate characters mentioned above.

History has straightened out most of the "incongruity" of previous volumes. In fact, Lowell retreats from the ground he has been occupying. "My old title, *Notebook,* was more accurate than I wished, i.e. the composition was jumbled. I hope this jumble or jungle is cleared—that I have cut the waste marble from the figure." [15] Aside from the ordinary process of selecting which of the old poems he wished to keep and which new poems he wished to add, Lowell has made two crucial alterations. First, he now arranges the poems not with reference to their actual composition but to chronological sequence. With certain exceptions, the poems begin at the dawn of human time, proceed through the Old Testament, Greek, Hellenic, and Roman worlds, the Middle Ages, and, finally, modern history, up to and including the present. Exceptions are safely encased within a powerful framework, so that allusions to Ulysses and Penelope in a sixties context is clearly a reflection on the past rather than a breaking down of time. Second, Lowell has excised the personal, private poems, and placed them in their own volume, *For Lizzie and Harriet*. Of special interest to us is the fact that the "Mexico" poem from which the lines about learning to live in history, that thing you cannot touch, appears in this "private" book. And this is perfectly suitable, since *History* makes history a thing you can, more or less, touch.

Here, we touch upon the first—but not the last—discordant

15. *History* (New York: Farrar, Straus and Giroux, 1973), p. 7.

note we have encountered. Until this point, we have read of a growing capacity to escape from the self, and from such constructs of the self as time and history. But the publication of *History*, which brings us nearly to the present, marks a definite pulling back from that position. We have heretofore celebrated the arrangement of poetry Lowell called first "jagged in pattern," then "intuitive in arrangement"[16] But we now find that that organization constitutes a "jumble." We must from this time forward be aware of the distinct possibility that we have been exploring not an ongoing movement, evolving steadily into the shape poetry will take in the future, but rather a finite probe, an exploration that would discover how far off a rational center the poet could move and still maintain his art. If poetry is the response of the total organism to experience, the response of both rational and non-rational centers, it may indeed be impossible to push poetry too far toward either extreme. Lowell, at least, seems to be retreating from what he perceives to be his own non-rational extreme. But in doing so he not only alerts us to the possible temporal boundaries of the approach to experience we have been studying, but also helps us to understand the precise nature of that approach. To the confusion between inner and outer worlds he reacts by dividing his work into public and private sectors; to the breakdown of the time-scheme he reacts by giving us history. But this only reminds us how successfully he accomplished what he must now adjust to the claims of the rational.

There is probably no better example in contemporary American literature of the audience's fascination with the life of a writer threatening to overwhelm its capacity to respond fairly to that writer's work than the case of Sylvia Plath. There is no need to do more than sketch in outline the life of this bright, gifted, attractive woman who killed herself one grey, winter morning in London, her head in the oven, her two small children in the next room. She was thirty years old. To reach that moment,

16. *Notebook 1967–68*, p. 159; *Notebook*, p. 262.

she had led a life that was on the one hand clearly promising, on the other, headed directly toward disaster. She had won a writing prize and been a guest editor for *Mademoiselle* while still a teenager (recorded fictionally in *The Bell Jar*), studied writing under Robert Lowell and with Anne Sexton, married successful British poet Ted Hughes, and forged her own considerable writing skills. However, her first distinct suicide attempt came close on the heels of that writing prize (and was also recorded in *The Bell Jar*); it was followed by others. Her marriage to Hughes had already broken up. Her poetry, although already published in book form in *The Colossus* (1960), was not considered exceptional. She was probably very much aware that a good deal of the attention she did receive was due as much to her being Hughes's wife as to her own work.

Although since her death the earlier poetry has been given the careful reading every young poet would like to have, and has generally been judged the work of a competent craftsman and promising poet, the truth is there are few poems written before the last months of her life that would have earned her an important place among contemporary American poets. But those last few months tell a different story, a story that has contributed significantly to the romanticizing of her life. Plath went through two periods of intense, maybe frenzied creativity, one in the fall of 1962, the other in the first week of February 1963 (she died February 11 of that year). Some of the poems are about suicide, some seem poised between life and death. It is understandable that the fact that she did finally kill herself, and that her major poems were written shortly before her death, almost in preparation for it, appeared to add legitimacy to her work, almost as if, it sometimes seems, her poems would lose most of their worth without the suicide to back them up. What would have happened, one wonders, if, as Sylvia Plath probably intended in this as in her other suicide attempts, she had been found in time to be saved?

Nonetheless, the reader of Confessional poetry has taken for granted the right to assume a special relationship between life and work, for the simple reason that the writer seems to insist that that relationship be emphasized. In a sense, this cannot be denied. However, we may still have the right to say that if there is an important relationship between life and work, it is not one to which we have become accustomed. The curious fact is that the reader of Confessional poetry needs less of a background to understand that work than the reader of most other poetry, if for no other reason than that the Confessional poet provides whatever information the reader should have. If we remember Lowell's remarks about *Life Studies*, we will recognize that there is no point in learning the "true" facts of the poet's life, since the poem is admittedly a selection and distortion made in the interests of creating a "real" version of the poet, in short, of creating a myth. It is the myth of the self, which reaches inward to the archetypal patterns of the collective unconscious, and outward to the shared experiences of the poet's society, rather than the objective actions of the arbitrarily isolated individual, that forms the focus of Confessional poetry.

In *The New Poets*, M. L. Rosenthal singles out Robert Lowell and Sylvia Plath for writing poems that place "the speaker himself at the center of the poem in such a way as to make his psychological vulnerability and shame an embodiment of his civilization."[17] While we may quarrel with the notion, implicit in that comment, that the poems operate through exposition of the author's pathology, the idea of the poet as embodiment of his civilization is worth following up. We can do no better than to turn to the more spectacular poems of *Ariel* (1965), which, in spite of Ted Hughes's claim that the poems were chosen arbitrarily,[18] surely contains almost all of the poems upon which Sylvia Plath's reputation must finally rest.

"Daddy" is a head-on encounter with the ambivalent feelings toward her father we might expect to find in a woman who both loved and feared him, and who was hindered in resolving those responses by his early death. Much of the poem's power comes from the fact that a complex of emotions that generally would

17. P. 79.

18. Note following title page of Sylvia Plath, *Winter Trees* (New York: Harper and Row, 1972).

be relegated to the unconscious is here consciously experienced; in Norman Brown's terms, what was previously repressed is now made conscious. "I have had to kill you,"[19] the poet asserts; part of her feels trapped by this necessity, but part of her gloats. She has finally evened the score with this awesome memory. A good deal of the poem is an evocation of the previous fears. So great is the burden of anxiety and guilt, she tried to kill herself, to "get back to" him. Then, Plath tells us how she has dealt with the problem of coming to terms with a man long dead. She married a man in his image, a man who "said" he was her father, and by killing him—literally by killing her need for him—she has killed her father as well. The poem concludes: "Daddy, daddy, you bastard, I'm through." It is shocking, even sick, if we identify as the source of the poet's voice ordinary areas of consciousness, but perfectly usual if it springs from an expanded conception of the self.

But those familiar with the poem will recognize that one of its most important components has been omitted: the imagery with which these feelings are expressed. Appropriately enough, most of the images are drawn from World War II, which in many respects may be understood as an externalization of nightmare corners of the psyche. "Ich, ich, ich, ich," Sylvia Plath cries, her tongue stuck in the barbed wire of her father's language. He is the quintessential German, the quintessential Nazi. And what is she? She is the Jew to his Nazi.

> *An engine, an engine*
> *Chuffing me off like a Jew.*
> *A Jew to Dachau, Auschwitz, Belsen.*
> *I began to talk like a Jew.*
> *I think I may well be a Jew.*

She returns to her "Aryan"-eyed "panzer-man," but this time not only insists that she is his victim, but confesses that she has been attracted to her role all along.

19. *Ariel* (London: Faber and Faber, 1965), p. 54.

Not God but a swastika
So black no sky could squeak through.
Every woman adores a Fascist,
The boot in the face, the brute
Brute heart of a brute like you.

When she can not get back to her tormenter, to kill the need
she had for him, she finds his duplicate, dressed "in black with
a Meinkampf look." At the end, the imagery changes its base.
Already referred to as a devil, her father now becomes a vam-
pire; her husband is the man who has drunk her blood for seven
years. But now this two-in-one model has a stake in his heart,
and the villagers—who never did like him—dance on his grave.

The story, the action of the poem, has been derived from what
is ordinarily the unconscious. The mode of perceiving, of understanding that action has been derived from the collective experience of the poet's society. It is fitting that the imagery at the
end shift to the world of the cinema, itself a mass medium, and
to the world of folklore and myth lurking behind it. It is finally
the villagers, that is, the poet in her identification with the collective unconscious within her, and her fellow members of her
civilization without her, that put an end to Daddy. In other
words, the breaking down of these barriers has been a source of
strength, not anguish, for the poet, enabling her to realize the
expanded selfhood which alone could free her from her father's
hold. A qualifying note must be added. Just as there is in the
rhythm of the poem an excitement that verges on hysteria, so
there is an anxiousness in the poet's assertion of freedom that
undermines if not its validity, at least its permanence. Creation
provides relief, but, for Sylvia Plath in any case, only death provides final relief.

In "Lady Lazarus," Plath takes on not the causes of her suicidal impulses, but explores the implications of her actions themselves: their impact on other people in her world. Her recognition that they do have impact should not be taken for granted.
She must now confront the fact that as well as being a victim of
the conditions that have made her wish to die, she is also a

manipulator, trading on her own torment. Consequently, the poem's irony is complex, directed, as was the case in Pound's "Hugh Selwyn Mauberley," partly at the protagonist, partly at the protagonist's audience.

The poem begins with the horror of returning from the grave, which she has been accomplishing every ten years. Then, the suicide attempts become a spectacle for "The peanut-crunching crowd" (*Ariel*, p. 17). This is "The big strip tease," and while there is a certain consciousness of herself as showman, as a performer, most of her contempt is directed toward the crowd that is attracted by her pitch. Toward the middle of the poem comes a dead serious moment, a description of what it "feels" like to be dead and come back; they "pick the worms off me like sticky pearls." Finally, the poet asserts that there is indeed "a price" to be paid for watching the show. "Do not think I underestimate your great concern," she says with bitter sarcasm to those who should care about her. She ends with a warning.

Out of the ash
I rise with my red hair
and I eat men like air.

Again, Plath draws upon the Second World War for the imagery with which to express her experience; nothing less will serve as concrete equivalent to her psychic torment, nothing less will free her from the burden of isolation. Her reborn skin is "Bright as a Nazi lampshade," her face is "Jew linen." As in "Daddy," she becomes the archetypal Jew, and though there may not, in fact, be any biographical justification for this identification, it is surely the appropriate myth, necessary in order to communicate to us what it feels like to be the "real" Sylvia Plath. After moving into the "show business" metaphor at the poem's center, she returns to the cencentration camp imagery with renewed intensity and bitterness. Her antagonist is referred to as Herr Doktor, Herr Enemy, Herr God, Herr Lucifer. He is—or they are—psychiatrist, husband, and father rolled up in one. She burns until there is nothing left except

A cake of soap,
A wedding ring,
A gold filling.

Not mentioned by name, her "Nazi" father lurks behind the scenes. He is her original tormenter; he, as the warnings that conclude this poem suggest, is the one she must destroy, whom she does destroy in "Daddy." So that the World War Two imagery provides links among several of the poems. More important, it provides external areas of experience that serve effectively to represent less concrete, inner states. Most important, however, is the completeness with which Plath identifies with aspects of that external experience, so that she does not seem to be saying that she is like a Jew as much as she seems to become the Jew; by reaching deeply within herself, she has found a place that is inhabited by others. The process is strikingly analagous to that suggested by Williams, fixing the particular with the universality of her own personality.

Plath does not confine her use of imagery drawn from the War to Germany and the concentration camp. When it is her own sense of guilt, rather than of victimization, that she wishes to confront, the War is still an appropriate source. The imagery of "Fever 103°" is, in fact, largely derived from Dante. The literal experience is an illness, a high fever, which becomes associated in the poet's mind with an adulterous relationship. The fever, then, becomes a purifying flame, as the poet moves from Hell to Paradise. In the middle of the poem, however, in the section that may well represent purgatory, Dante's leopard, symbol of the sins of incontinence, is destroyed by the atomic bomb.

Devilish leopard!
Radiation turned it white
And killed it in an hour.

Greasing the bodies of adulterers
Like Hiroshima ash and eating in.
The sin. The sin.   (ARIEL, p. 58)

This is the essence of Sylvia Plath's method. The sense of particular guilt is exorcised by means of universal guilt, which Plath has little difficulty finding within herself. In one sense, the confusion of sexual guilt and guilt resulting from the dropping of the atomic bomb may be thought of as "crazy." And yet, this craziness, this access to a feeling that makes no rational sense but nonetheless exists in the poet's unconscious, again proves to be a source of strength, a temporary stay against confusion.

However, it did not provide permanence. In fact, the real difficulty with the expanded, fluid self that pervades Plath's poetry seems to be the tension involved in maintaining a separate identity whose boundaries are continually merging with encompassing realities. The temptation to relax is enormous. In "Ariel," for example, she becomes one with her horse, then with all of nature, as she "unpeels" the qualities that distinguish her from the rest of being, and races "suicidal" into "the cauldron of morning" (p. 37). Here, at least, we seem to be approaching that extreme effacement of the ego which threatens not simply poetry, but life itself.

There are still many questions about the nature of the creative process that produces this poetry. Did Plath have an expanded sense of self, or was her extraordinary access to the materials of her unconscious precisely what constitutes madness? Did she provoke anguish for the sake of writing poems, or were the poems her way of stemming her anguish? No matter what the answer to these questions, the reader's responsiveness to the configurations of her poetry must be based on a willingness to see the individual not as an isolated being, but rather one who contains within himself universality, and to perceive the boundaries that effect that isolation as less than permanent.

If Lowell's testing of the traditional self consists chiefly of obliterating the distinction between private and public worlds, and Plath's of unifying individual unconscious and collective myth, John Berryman's contribution is nothing less than a head-on assault on the notion of a single, consistent personality.

In the same essay in which he professes to have less confidence than he had once possessed in continuity of personality, Berryman has some interesting remarks to make about an early piece, "The Ball Poem." Using ambiguous pronouns, shifting back and forth from "he" to "I," "The poet himself is both left out and put in; the boy does and does not become him and we are confronted with a process which is at once a process of life and a process of art."[20] For the first time in our discussion, we encounter a poet who admits to an awareness of a lack of clear-cut boundaries between the observer and the object observed, and who associates this lack with the idea of discontinuous personality.

Homage to Mistress Bradstreet (1956) represents the first use by Berryman in a major work of his rather flexible sense of personality. As a note tells us, the poem begins with the voice of the living poet, and in the fourth stanza "modulates" into the voice of the dead woman.[21] In addition, the writer "interrupts" his creation several times during the course of the poem, engages in a dialogue with, and finally takes over again to conclude the poem. It is possible to understand these shifts of personality and speaking voice by saying that Bradstreet is after all a projection of Berryman's psyche, an *anima* that embodies the modern poet's struggle toward spiritual wholeness, much in the manner of Theodore Roethke's "Meditations of an Old Woman," in which the poet speaks through his mother's voice. However, Roethke is consistent in his use of the persona's voice; there are no shifts back and forth. A more apt comparison may be to Leonard Cohen's novel *Beautiful Losers* (1966), in which the narrator is in love with the dead Indian saint Catherine Tekakwitha. In Cohen's book, as in Berryman's poem, the relationship between live author and dead woman is rendered imaginatively believable by the lack of clear boundaries between characters. If there is no spatial integrity of personality, why should there be temporal integrity?

20. "Changes," p. 98.

21. *Homage to Mistress Bradstreet and Other Poems* (New York: Farrar, Straus and Giroux, 1968), p. 30.

John Berryman's major work, the one that is also the principal monument to his sense of personality, is his *Dream Songs* (*77 Dream Songs*, 1964; *His Toy, His Dream, His Rest,* 1968). In some ways, *The Dream Songs* is another one of those poems of the sort we have come to expect from modern American poets: it takes the shape of the poet's experience; it is a running commentary on the poet's psychic life, in the manner of *Notebook 1967–68*, lacking the traditional sense of unity that once was the first and obvious requisite of a long poem. And although it is a far more personal poem than the *Cantos* or its descendants in that it explores the inner life of the poet directly, *Dream Songs,* again like *Notebook,* is almost encyclopedic in its attempt to encompass the totality of the experience of the poet in his society, over a given period of time.

Before examining the poems, we ought to look at Berryman's own comments about the persona of *Dream Songs*. In a note to *77 Dream Songs,* he says: "Many opinions and errors in the Songs are to be referred not to the character Henry, still less to the author, but to the title of the work." [22] From this we learn of the poet's insistence that Henry is not he, and that the logic, time-sense, and perception of reality in general, will be those of dreams rather than objective reality. In other words, Henry, whoever he is, is the center of consciousness of the poem, but his unconscious, or *a* unconscious, has become a full partner in the poem. in fact, we might say that Henry is the poet's name for his consciousness, not to be confused with the total self of which it forms but a small part.

In *His Toy, His Dream, His Rest,* by now responding to critics who went "desperately astray," Berryman goes into greater detail about Henry.

> The poem then, whatever its wide cast of characters, is essentially about an imaginary character (not the poet, not me) named Henry, a white American in early middle age sometimes in blackface, who has suffered an irreversible loss and talks about himself sometimes in the first person, sometimes in the third, sometimes even in the

22. *77 Dream Songs* (New York: Farrar, Straus and Giroux, 1964), p. viii.

second; he has a friend, never named, who addresses him as Mr.
Bones and variants thereof.[23]

Whether the unnamed friend is or is not actually part of Henry,
the intended multiplicity of perspective is at once evident.
Switching from first, to third, to second persons, Berryman, or
Henry, applies the techniques of "The Ball Poem" and *Homage
to Mistress Bradstreet* to *The Dream Songs*. Of special interest
is the force with which Berryman denies that he is the persona
of the poem. "Not the poet, not me," he insists. But this is ambiguous. Does Berryman mean simply to intensify his denial by
means of redundancy, or is he making a real distinction between the poet in him and himself. That would leave us at the
least three people involved in the composition of the poem: Berryman, the poet, and Henry. This does not take into account
Henry's alternate name of Mr. Bones or the unnamed friend.
For most poets, this would not be a probable interpretation. But
in the case of Berryman, who has already dealt with a dual persona in *Homage,* and who in so many places leaves traces of his
belief in a multiple, non-continuous self, it is clearly a reasonable representation of the sense of reality the poet attempts to
capture in the poem.

Berryman's solution to the formal problems of his work is, as I
have already suggested, similar to Lowell's in *Notebook
1967–68*. In each case, there is a uniform number of lines,
which is generally observed but occasionally modified; in each
case, there are scattered rhyme schemes that are frequently altered or ignored. As for the differences, while Lowell chooses
the fourteen lines of the sonnet, Berryman uses three stanzas of
six lines each; Lowell uses basically blank verse, while Berryman is more variable, and very often makes the third and
sixth line of each stanza shorter than the rest, although there is
no consistent pattern; and finally, Berryman is much more devoted to rhyme than Lowell, although his continual employment
of off-rhymes somewhat blunts the effect. The point is this:

23. *His Toy, His Dream, His Rest* (New York: Farrar, Straus and Giroux,
1968), p. ix.

both Lowell and Berryman are strongly attracted to stricter forms, the sign of the rational consciousness asserting its control of the materials of the poem. But both must have the flexibility to undermine that conscious control at will, somewhat like Williams in his development of the variable foot. And both Lowell and Berryman succeed in limiting the effect of the forms they suggest by making them part of a much longer poem that, in Pound's phrase, has form as a tree has form, not, like the components of the poem, like a vase.

As Berryman himself suggests in his note to the second installment of *The Dream Songs,* quoted above, the poems are concerned with loss. But the principal manifestation of that loss throughout the sequence, particularly the first three books (77 *Dream Songs*), is the guilt Henry so pervasively feels. In Song 29, the burden is so heavy that in a hundred years he "could not make good" (p. 33). What it is precisely that Henry has done is not so easy to fathom, not even for Henry. One of the strongest moments in the entire poem occurs when, in that same Song, Henry tries to search out his crime.

> *But never did Henry, as he thought he did,*
> *end anyone and hacks her body up*
> *and hide the pieces, where they may be found.*
> *He knows: he went over everyone, & nobody's missing.*
> *Often he reckons, in the dawn, them up.*
> *Nobody is ever missing.*

Perhaps the offense was sexual in nature; it is a sex crime he fantasizes, and there are other Songs, Song 4, for example, where Henry has to struggle against illicit sexual impulses ("only the fact of her husband & four other people / kept me from springing on her"—p. 6). However, even if we agree on the basis of inconclusive evidence that Henry's guilt is sexual, we find that the areas of experience made available by Berryman are so numerous as to preclude precision. We do not know if the guilt is fact or fantasy, psychological or moral. It could be anything from an adulterous relationship—Berryman does describe an affair in his *Sonnets* (1967)—to an unresolved Oedipal conflict; it most certainly could be both.

The Freudian interpretation is especially tempting, however, because it makes the link between guilt—over desiring the mother—and loss—the necessity of relinquishing her. On the other hand, the material lends itself equally well to an existential reading. Guilt here is the anxiety over separation from the rest of creation, the terror of being a finite individual alone in a limitless universe, and loss is the intuitive recollection of the state of being at one with the universe. What is certain is the sense of guilt and the expectation that retribution will be exacted. As Henry himself puts it at the start of Song 76, "Henry's Confession":

> *Nothing very bad happen to me lately.*
> *How you explain that?*   (p. 83)

Perhaps the unnamed friend has the only coherent answer worth making. He says, in Song 62, "—Mr Bones, we all brutes & fools" (p. 69). Is there any need to search further than our own capacity to do harm, which we have most likely exercised, to explain Henry's guilt?

In Song 40, Henry dons blackface to speak more directly of his sense of loss, his loneliness. It is frightening to see the combers going out to sea, and "to know they're goin somewhere but not me" (p. 44). Here, loss is identified as death, that final and, from the point of the discrete individual, total loss. Death is indeed a persistent presence in 77 *Dream Songs*. Sometimes, as in Song 21, Henry is appalled by all the dead; sometimes Death is personified, for example, as a "German expert" in Song 41; sometimes, perhaps as a form of magic to ward off what he most dreads, as in Songs 26 and 46, he fantasizes his own death. Some Songs, like 18, "A Strut for Roethke," memorialize Berryman's colleagues, for death is not only a constant participant in the poet's psychic life but also an event in the real world.

But what is simply a dominant theme in the first three books of *The Dream Songs* becomes an overwhelming obsession in the last four books, *His Toy, His Dream, His Rest.* In this respect, Song 153 is typical of this portion of the sequence. In it, Berryman declares Henry "cross with god who has wrecked this generation," preying first on Roethke, Richard Blackmur, Randall Jarrell, and then Delmore Schwartz, while "In between he gorged on Sylvia Plath."[24] Berryman turns out elegies the way Saul Bellow's Herzog turns out letters to the dead; in addition to those already mentioned, Robert Frost, Wallace Stevens, William Carlos Williams, Ernest Hemingway, John F. Kennedy, and Yvor Winters pass before Henry's attention in a kind of procession of the newly dead. And Henry himself becomes part of this procession when every poem in Book IV is labeled "Op. Posth."

It should be clear by now that from Henry's point of view, and most likely from Berryman's as well, the situation is desperate. Shunning his isolation, yet terrified at the thought of the impending dissolution of his individuality, Berryman finds untenable the stance of the discrete consciousness attempting to give shape to the abyss. More than any of the writers we have considered so far—including Sylvia Plath, who is far more attracted to death than Berryman—he is driven by psychic necessity to expand the boundaries of the self, and, when possible, to obliterate those boundaries. In fact, it seems as if Berryman is intent on obliterating that very point of view of Henry's that is so hard to take.

We have already mentioned the use of several voices in the Songs, all of which seem to be component parts of Berryman, if not of Henry, and Henry's own frequent use of blackface to express the multiplicity and discontinuity of his personality. We may notice as well the variety of epithets applied to Henry even when he speaks in his own voice. He is at various times "huffy," "careful," "horrible," "servant," "gross," "bitter," "subtle," "seedy," "lonely," and "mortal" Henry, to mention some of those adjectives which indeed serve as epithets, and are therefore generalizations. In addition, Henry is addressed by such names

24. *His Toy, His Dream, His Rest*, p. 82.

as "Henry Pussy-cat," "Ol' Marster," and a slew of variations on "Bones." Henry is all of these moods and characteristics; but to Berryman, such words as mood and characteristic are disguises for the discontinuity we wish to cover up. "I stalk my mirror down this corridor / my pieces litter" (*His Toy . . .* , p. 124), Henry, aware of his multiplicity, says in Song 195; all the pieces kneel together and scream. In Song 201, we are give a look at the discreteness of perception and thought that leads to the discreteness of each "personality": "Hung by a thread more moments instant Henry's mind / supersubtle, which he knew blunt & empty & incurious. . . ." (*His Toy*, p. 130).

"A dream is a panorama / of the whole mental life" (*His Toy*, p. 259), Henry says in Song 327. And that is also a reasonable description of *The Dream Songs*. In Song 16, Berryman gives us both method and content of the *Songs*:

> *Henry's pelt was put on sundry walls*
> *where it did much resemble Henry and*
> *them persons was delighted.*   (p. 18)

The pelt may be thought of as the individual Song, displayed for our enjoyment; the surreal image, the fantasy made real, touches our own sense that what is real and what is rational do not always coincide. And it is ultimately this other than rational, other than conscious level upon which *The Dream Songs* speaks to us; it is meant to assuage the anguish experienced by the conscious self when it becomes aware of the isolation and finiteness of the human condition by appealing to that part of us that participates in the wholeness of experience rather than the rational core.

> *These Songs are not meant to be understood, you*
> *understand.*
> *They are only meant to terrify & comfort.* (*His Toy*, p. 298)

To summarize our conclusions to this point, we may say both Objectism and Confessional poetry abandon the traditional self as a perspective from which reality may be viewed and organized. For the most part, Objectism is, like Marshall McLuhan, more concerned with the perception of outer reality, with replacing the linearity of abstraction by concrete juxtaposition, while Confessional poetry, like Norman O. Brown, is more concerned with inner boundaries, with making conscious much that is now repressed. However, we have seen that Objectist poets make frequent appeal to the mythical patterns that speak for the unconscious, and that Confessional poets make far more use of techniques of juxtaposition than is generally supposed. It may well be that the taking of one or the other of these two stances implies an implicit acceptance of its opposite number. It is, after all, the fact that these relationships exist that enables us to see the underlying unity of contemporary American poetry in the face of its obvious diversity.

CHAPTER FIVE

Rules and Exceptions

IT can be legitimately argued
that Objectism and Confessional poetry are the two dominant
forces in post-war American poetry. As different as they may appear to be—and in many respects are—they share a common
significant characteristic: the abandonment of the ego as the
necessary perspective from which reality must be apprehended.
We can therefore assert that this shift in perspective constitutes
a major element in contemporary American poetry. How pervasive it is has yet to be determined. The working out of a thesis
in all its details can be tedious, and it is probably unnecessary to
subject all manifestations of contemporary poetry to close analysis. But it will nonetheless be useful to sketch out briefly the
place of the more important poetic schools in the scheme of
things. And, unless we are prepared to make the unlikely claim
that *all* contemporary American poetry has abandoned the "ego-
position," we must pay some attention to the exceptions, to see
how they affect our argument.

Of the Beat Generation poets who came to prominence during
the fifties, few have proved to have much staying power. The
obvious example of a Beat poet who has endured is Allen Ginsberg, and in his case at least, there is no difficulty at all in
seeing his work as the product of the new view of the self we
have been discussing.

In technique, Ginsberg, who came to poetic maturity under
the strong influence of William Carlos Williams, is clearly in the
Objectist category. His lines are breath units in the tradition of

Whitman, and as prescribed by Charles Olson. What is not generally known, however, is the fact that Ginsberg consciously practiced the precise aesthetic principles developed by Ezra Pound and the Imagists, and that he expressed those principles in terms that Ford Madox Ford and T. E. Hulme, as well as Pound, would have found especially congenial.

> . . . I had the idea, perhaps overrefined, that by the unexplainable, unexplained nonperspective line, that is, juxtaposition of one *word* against another, a *gap* between the two words—like the space gap in the canvas—there'd be a gap between the two words which the mind would fill in with the sensation of existence.[1]

In subject matter, Ginsberg cannot easily be characterized, but in much of his poetry, and most particularly and effectively in one of his major works, *Kaddish,* he is clearly Confessional in his concerns. In that poem, the madness of his mother, Naomi, which clearly touches off resonant chords in himself, is a distortion that brings into clearer focus the nature of reality. And Ginsberg adds to his attack on the conscious, rational self a mode of experiencing the world that none of the poets we have to this point considered has taken seriously and systematically: mysticism. Here, of course, the self is manifestly illusion, and harmony triumphs decisively over divisiveness. Nonetheless, Ginsberg is a poet, and in poets harmony cannot persistently and completely prevail, lest poetry itself disappear. In "Psalm III," he demonstrates that his mysticism, at least, must have concrete embodiment: "I feel on your Name like a cockroach on a crumb—this cockroach is holy."[2]

Of the San Francisco Renaissance, little need to be said beyond the fact that it constituted a unification of Beat Generation poetry with that of the Black Mountain School. Black Mountain was the experimental college in North Carolina to which Charles Olson, who became rector in the late forties, attracted such poets as Robert Creeley, Robert Duncan, Edward

---

1. *Writers at Work: The Paris Review Interviews,* Third Series (New York: Viking, 1967), p. 295.
2. *Reality Sandwiches* (San Francisco: City Lights Books, 1963), p. 62.

Dorn, and Joel Oppenheimer, all of whom were crucially influenced by Olson's Projectivist poetics. Duncan, as well as Kenneth Rexroth, Kenneth Patchen, and other poets working in open forms were in San Francisco in 1953 when Lawrence Ferlinghetti founded the City Lights Bookstore. With the notorious publication of Ginsberg's *Howl* in 1956, the "movement" was under way and another stretch of poetic territory staked out for poets who had abandoned the conscious self as exclusive poetic voice.

At the other end of the country, also in the fifties, another conglomerate of poets was taking shape: the New York Poets. Frank O'Hara, John Ashbery, and Kenneth Koch met at Harvard, and all came to live in New York, attracted by the worlds of theater and, especially, art, that made their capitol in the city. They became the center of a group that included James Schuyler and Edward Field, although the association was too loose to be called a movement in the sense that, say, Imagism was a movement.

The problem of the aesthetic principles of the New York Poets is, since they are intimately bound up with the aesthetics of the visual arts, too complex to be taken up in detail here. But these writers do hold a rather general allegiance to poetry in open forms, to juxtaposition of images rather than to the sequential arrangement of those images according to rational plan. They should be distinguished from Projectivist poets because of the strong and manifest influence of the literary and artistic principles of Symbolism, Surrealism, and Dada; but clearly, none of those approaches to experience invites increased control of the rational.

One of the more interesting demonstrations of the close relationship between the work of the New York Poets and the tradition developed by Pound and his admirers came about almost accidentally. When Frank O'Hara died in 1966, he had published only a few slender volumes; much of his poetry that had appeared in periodicals was uncollected. In addition, as it turned out, a substantial number of poems had never been published at all. Although this is not in itself remarkable, when

Donald M. Allen edited *The Collected Poems of Frank O'Hara* in 1971 and included, in chronological order, every poem of O'Hara's he could lay his hands on, it became clear not only that the uncollected poems were of more or less the same quality of those collected, but the unpublished poems as well were of comparable quality. The fact was that O'Hara had never treated poems as the concentrated representations of rationally conceived visions of reality, thereby gathering into themselves by centripetal force vast stretches of experience; poems were rather perceptual acts that belonged to the moment of perception, to the present, and which recorded experience rather than organized it. As a consequence, O'Hara seems to have been rather relaxed about collecting poems whose arrangements would be, except for the principles of tone upon which he seemed to operate, arbitrary in any case. When Allen, however, made the comprehensive collection, choosing chronology as the least distorting plan of organization, a work emerged that possessed a strange unity. It is, to be sure, a unity we once could not have recognized. But after the *Cantos, Paterson,* the *Maximus Poems, Notebook 1967–68,* and *The Dream Songs,* it is possible to think of *The Collected Poems of Frank O'Hara* as a single poem. Because the individual poems do not bear the weight of comprehensive vision, the poems as a whole are able to cohere and become the embodiment of a man's experience of the world that is perceptual and total rather than cognitive and selective.

Although less publicized as a movement than the groupings already mentioned, Deep Imagism can claim some of the most distinguished poets writing today, including Robert Bly, James Wright, Louis Simpson, and James Dickey. In fact, the "movement"—and, as in each case, we must be uncomfortable with labels that if taken seriously rather than as a convenience can be misleading—centers on two magazines: *Trobar,* edited by Robert Kelly, and with which Jerome Rothenberg and Diane Wakoski were associated; and *The Fifties* (which has changed its name with each new decade), edited by Robert Bly, and with which Wright, Simpson, and Dickey have been associated.

What draws these writers together is their belief in the primacy of the image in the writing of poetry. This would seem to be a simple instance of the influence of Imagism, which would scarcely require further comment. However, this is anything but the case, since Projectivism, the direct descendant of Imagism, and even Imagism itself, are the chief antagonists of the Deep Imagists.

In part, it is a question of responding to what some poets felt was an overemphasis on technique. Poetry was becoming too mechanical; for example, Charles Olson's insistence on the syllable as the basic unit of the poem seemed excessive. "The fundamental rhythm of the poem," Kelly wrote in 1961, is the rhythm of the images; their textures, their contents, offer supplementary rhythms."[3] And although this indeed sounds very much like an appeal for a return to Imagism, Bly had written two years earlier; "Even the Imagists were misnamed: they did not write in images from the unconscious, as Lorca or Neruda, but in simple pictures such as 'petals on a wet black bough. . . .' "[4] In the light of such remarks, it is almost unnecessary to quote the following passage from Robert Bly's "Waking from Sleep" to be aware of the relationship of Deep Imagism to Surrealism:

Inside the veins there are navies setting forth,
Tiny explosions at the water lines,
And seagulls weaving in the wind of the salty blood.[5]

Like the Confessional poets, the Deep Imagists challenge arbitrary distinctions between conscious and unconscious perceptions of the world; like them, they discover universality by carrying out subjectivity to its extreme conclusion. Where they differ from the Confessionals, however, is in the fact that they are less interested in probing the inner sources of behavior than in forg-

3. *Trobar* 2 (1961).   4. *The Fifties,* 3 (1959), 8.
5. *Silence in the Snowy Fields* (Middletown, Conn.: Wesleyan University Press, 1962), p. 13.

ing perceptual links between inner and outer landscapes. Kelly, in fact, writes, "Poetry, like dream reality, is the juncture of the experienced with the never-experienced. Like waking reality, it is the fulfillment of the imagined and the unimagined."[6] This is not unrelated to Pound's wish "to record the precise instant when a thing outward and objective transforms itself, or darts into a thing inward and subjective."[7] It is precisely in the moment of juncture, and in the breaking down of the boundaries that create those junctures, that poets as different as those we have been discussing find their common ground.

A final group large enough to demand consideration would seem to form an exception to the rule: the New Black Poets. Committed to the aesthetics of social responsibility, they reject the more formal of the problems we have been discussing as dangerously beside the point and are actually in the business of strengthening rather than escaping from the ego. But here we must be careful not to be trapped by words. For these Black Poets are involved in their own attempt to redefine the self. And if they have any common ground at all with the basically white poets we have been discussing, it is in their rejection of the traditional, white, western ego, with its impulses to bind and dominate, and its bias in favor of the abstract. In addition, their work constitutes the most forceful attempt to replace the strictly literate with the oral in contemporary American poetry.

In fact, the New Black Poets are very much in sympathy with Norman Brown's perception that genital tyranny is the bodily equivalent to colonialism and oppression in general, while polymorphous perversity is equivalent to fraternity and democracy, although they would hardly analyze the problem in that way. And they would have a similar unrecorded affinity for Marshall McLuhan's sense that the tyranny of sight leads to the impulse to abstract from and dominate the perceptual universe. So in spite of the fact that relatively clear-cut, rationally shaped, con-

6. Kelly, in *Trobar* 2 (1961).
7. J. P. Sullivan, ed., *Ezra Pound: A Critical Anthology* (Baltimore, Md.: Penguin, 1970), p. 34.

sciously apprehended "messages" emerge from much of their poetry, these writers do not constitute a repudiation of the dominant tendencies we have been observing.

Although an analysis of movements is of limited use in explicating the work of a given poet, it does give some idea of the fundamental assumptions made by the poets operating within a specific tradition. And it seems clear that to the extent to which these movements are in fact representative of contemporary American poetry, they confirm the thesis that the defining characteristic of this poetry is the escape from the self. However, all poets are not even in some remote way members of specific schools. It would be impossible to examine the work of each of these unaligned poets, nor, if we could, would we find that they all fell within the tradition that is the subject of this study. Nonetheless, to demonstrate that this tradition is represented beyond the limits of particular movements and schools, it would be useful to examine, albeit briefly, the work of two poets without specific affiliations: A. R. Ammons and Mark Strand.

In an article devoted to these poets, whom he believes to be among the finest of his own generation, Harold Bloom asserts that "They represent two permanent . . . strains óf American Romanticism that cannot be reconciled with one another. . . ."[8] Ammons is a poet of light; Strand of darkness. We are reminded, although Bloom does not draw this particular analogy, of Hart Crane's attempts to reconcile Whitman and Poe in *The Bridge*. Our own bridge, for use in effecting a similar reconciliation, may turn out to be precisely that erosion of the boundaries of the self we have been discussing.

In fact, in "Corsons Inlet," Ammons is more explicit than any Projectivist in announcing his dedication to this task.

In nature there are few sharp lines: . . .

I have reached no conclusions, have erected no boundaries,
shutting out and shutting in, separating inside

8. "Dark and Radiant Peripheries: Mark Strand and A. R. Ammons," *The Southern Review*, 8, N. S. (January 1972), 134.

from outside: I have
drawn no lines. . . .[9]

Corsons Inlet (1965) was an early book. But Ammons' chief
theme has remained the same and has even been worked out in
more detail in recent works, as, for example, in this passage
from *Sphere* (1974):

the heights and depths somewhere join in a near-complete
fizzle of the discrete: on either side well-boundaried
by the impassable, our selves float here, as

safely as duration allows, time in its stew mixing as much as
unmixing: I could not say, then, that the earthworm is not
my radical cousin, and I could not say that my veins
      entering

along the cell walls disresemble the transportive leaf:
I mean, if one speaks of mysticism, it makes good science,
which is the best part of science. . . .[10]

We may note in passing a crucial component of the approach to
reality under consideration: that it takes what could once be assumed only mystically as a "scientific" truth; the expansive self
is not a special case, a difficult to attain mode of aprehending
reality, but rather the ordinary state of things.

Although Mark Strand has never been particularly associated
with the Confessional poets, perhaps because of the absence of
detailed gossip in his work—he deals with raw emotion rather
than placing it in the context of its presumed cause—the similarities in their approaches to experience are testimony to the
fact that confession is the least essential characteristic of Confessional poetry. The sense of a fragmented, tenuous self per-

9. *Collected Poems 1961–71* (New York: Norton, 1972), pp. 148–49. (The poem
"Corsons Inlet," originally appeared in the book *Corsons Inlet,* 1965.)
10. *Sphere: The Form of a Motion* (New York: Norton, 1974), p. 15.

vades his work, as it does the work of the Confessionals. Theodore Roethke and John Berryman in particular come to mind when Strand writes:

> *In a field*
> *I am the absence*
> *of field.*
> *This is*
> *always the case.*
> *Wherever I am*
> *I am what is missing.*

In "The Man in the Mirror," the poet's reflection becomes a symbol of his fragmented self; and the surrealistic imagery reinforces this attack on a simplistic conception of the self:

> *Your suit floating, your hair*
> *moving like eel grass*
> *in a shallow bay, you drifted*
> *out of the mirror's room, through the hall*
>
> *and into the open air.*[11]

However, it is by no means the contention of this study that *all* poets writing in the contemporary period have abandoned the traditional self. But if our thesis, that this abandonment is in fact characteristic of the period, is correct, we ought to be able to find certain patterns in the work of the exceptions to the rule. And we can begin searching for those patterns at the point at which our investigations originally started, the poem's formal dimensions.

We return to the distinction made by Ezra Pound when he was trying to provide a justification for a form that no longer requires justification: free verse. Some poems have form as a

---

11. "Keeping Things Whole" and "The Man in the Mirror," in *Reasons for Moving* (New York: Atheneum, 1968), pp. 40, 44.

vase has form, some as a tree. If the form represented by the vase indeed stands for rationally conceived form, while that represented by the tree stands for intuitively perceived form, then there ought to be some sort of relationship between meter and stanzaic form and confidence in the rational self on the one hand, and intuitive rhythms and organic form and a loss of confidence in that self on the other. While it is difficult to draw generalizations, some such sort of relationship does, in fact, seem to exist.

To begin with, among the poets we have been discussing, the Projectivists fairly consistently abjure metrical and stanzaic strictures. The Confessionals, however, operate both with and without such discipline, and therefore should be considered before an examination of the consistently formal poets is made.

Theodore Roethke is probably the most interesting case of all. Roethke begin as a formal poet in *Open House* (1941), but as soon as he had learned to delve beneath the rational surface of things, in *The Lost Son and Other Poems* (1948), he turned to organic rhythms, to free verse in a variety of manifestations. However, Roethke did not stay unwaveringly with free verse; he shifted back and forth, according to which mode he felt was most appropriate to the particular poem. And a pattern of usage does, in fact, emerge. When Roethke is exploring the psychology of self, as he does in the Greenhouse Poems, the poems of *Praise to the End!* (1951), "Meditations of an Old Woman," and "North American Sequence," he chooses open forms, rhythms dictated by the emotional energy of the lines. However, when he attempts to convert those same impulses into theology, or at least some religious or philosophical context as he does in "Love Poems" and "Sequence Sometimes Metaphysical," Roethke uses iambic meters (predominantly pentameter) and clearly defined stanzaic patterns, end-stopping his lines to emphasize the effect. In other words, when he is fitting his feelings into a rationally understandable system he uses stock forms; when the nonrational is allowed to find its own path, he uses organic forms. An interesting effect of this dichotomy, one that helps confirm it, is that the "mystical" experiences in Roethke's work that are the expression of the total organism, including the nonrational, as, for example, in the conclusion of "The Lost Son," are joyful; while those that are the expressions of rational consciousness, like "In a Dark Time," are filled with terror. And indeed, it is precisely, and only, the rational consciousness that has something to fear in the individual's recognition of his participation in the totality of being.

In the work of Robert Lowell, a similar distinction can be made. The early poems of *Lord Weary's Castle* (1946), written in the wake of the poet's conversion to Catholicism, with clearly metaphysical leanings, follow conventional forms. But the poems of *Life Studies* (1959), written by a lapsed Catholic, exploring and challenging the boundaries of the self, frequently break loose of stanzaic and metrical restraint.

It is not always possible to make such generalizations. It is nonetheless true that most poets of the post-war period who have not given themselves over totally to open forms have at least been affected by them, so that there is a tension between strict and flexible form throughout their work. And the gradual movement of a W. S. Merwin or a Louis Simpson from rational to organic forms is the rule rather than the exception.

Nonetheless, it is still possible to identify poets who throughout their careers have maintained a devotion to conventional form, and who, although they might indeed occasionally lapse into freer verse, can always return to older patterns without having their work exhibit the tension so often produced by the encounter of conflicting poetic possibilities. However, if we begin to draw up a list of those poets, including, say, Delmore Schwartz, Karl Shapiro, and Randall Jarrell, we notice that each of them possesses an Existentialist bias—though not necessarily a formal allegiance to that philosophical position—which we may for purposes of our discussion define as the assertion, by virtue of the absurd, of the integrity of the self in the face of its manifest disintegration.

This is a sweeping generalization, the full demonstration of which could hardly avoid becoming an overly long digression. Even so, it is easy enough to look at some passages characteristic of these poets, which differ substantially in form and content from the work of the poets who have dominated this study. We can in this way at least illustrate and clarify our characterization of the former group, if not prove it conclusively. Randall Jarrell, for example, in "The Knight, Death, and the Devil," says:

> *The death of his own flesh, set up outside him;*
> *The flesh of his own soul, set up outside him—*
> *Death and the devil, what are these to him?*
> *His being accuses him—and yet his fate is firm*
> *In resolution, in absolute persistence;*
> *The folds of smiling do for steadiness;*
> *The face of its own fate*—a man does what he must—
> *And the body underneath it says:* I am.[12]

Here as elsewhere in Jarrell, the theme is the assertion of the self in the face of its ultimate—and in this case—impending dissolution. Rather than flee that self, as the poets we have been considering seem to do, the Knight will cling to it for all he is worth; and that is precisely the ground of his dignity, his nobility.

Especially in his later poems, Delmore Schwartz appears on the verge of abandoning the rhymes and meters that characterize his work, of breaking through the tyranny of the self. Robert Lowell was quite perceptive when, by placing him in the quartet of writers with whom he could identify, he made Schwartz a kind of ancestor of the Confessional mode in verse. Nonetheless, he did hang on; and we might profitably compare Schwartz's consequent attitude toward time with that of the writers less committed to the ego. "Calmly We Walk Through This April Day" concludes:

> *Time is the school in which we learn,*
> *Time is the fire in which we burn.*

12. *The Complete Poems* (New York: Farrar, Straus and Giroux, 1969), p. 22.

And in "Time's Dedication," Schwartz writes,

We cannot stand still: time is dying,
We are dying: Time is farewell! [13]

Of course, this theme is as old as lyric poetry itself, and there is nothing strange or original in Schwartz's use of it. What I wish to point out is the fact that it is for the most part absent from the work of contemporary poets, and that it should not be surprising to find one of its rare appearances coinciding with equally rare commitment to the self.

Karl Shapiro is in many ways the most interesting of these formal, self-affirming poets, since his work has moved from the rigors of meter and rhyme to the "freedom" of prose, without really resting in the realm of free verse, which is a kind of compromise between the two extremes. Shapiro is also a convenient poet for the purposes of this study, for he is one of the few who articulates as his intention the defense of the ego. In his work, the Jew, for example, becomes symbolic of the attempt to preserve the self in the modern world. As I have written elsewhere,

> A metaphor begins to emerge in which Jew comes to represent a particular quality of mind, one that is intimately related to the creative process. We are dealing with that aspect of consciousness that is conscious of itself, that is, in fact, obsessed with itself; it is "the primitive ego of the human race," attempting to survive against a "background of Nothing." [14]

In a poem like "The Leg," Shapiro displays his preoccupation with the difficulty of defining the self, with the dichotomies between mind and body, between self and outer world. As the soldier becomes aware of his loss, he recognizes the problems inherent in any effort to isolate the self:

For the leg is wondering where he is. . . .
He is its injury, the leg is his orphan,
He must cultivate the mind of the leg. . . . [15]

13. *Selected Poems* (New York: New Directions, 1967), pp. 67, 77.
14. *Contemporary American-Jewish Literature,* ed. Irving Malin (Bloomington: Indiana University Press, 1973), p. 213.
15. *Poems of a Jew* (New York: Random House, 1958), p. 32.

What is especially characteristic of Shapiro is the fact that loss becomes the occasion of definition of the self; in fact, without loss, without negation, there could be no individuation, no conception of selfhood.

This theme is reasserted in the sequence, "Adam and Eve," in which man's original sense of union with nature is shattered by human access to the world of thought and self-consciousness: "Thinking became a garden of its own" (p. 62). Adam and Eve leave Eden "gladly," for the loss of eternity makes possible the pleasures and achievement of time. Sexuality becomes, paradoxically, a way of reestablishing the semblance of harmony through the exploitation of separateness. And, finally, the original garden itself becomes most beautiful now that it is out of reach. We see

Eden ablaze with fires of red and gold,
The garden dressed for dying in cold flame.　　　　(p. 69)

Loss allows us to define the self; and this spiritual confidence is reflected in the formal dimensions of the sequence, which display total mastery of regular metrical and stanzaic patterns.

It is no coincidence, then, that when Shapiro turns to the prose poems of *The Bourgeois Poet* (1964), leaving behind his allegiance to rigorous pattern, he also launches an explicit attack on the possibilities of maintaining the self's integrity:

> The prophets say to Know Thyself: I say it can't be done. . . . Man is mostly involuntary. Consciousness is only a tiny part of us. . . . Those poets who study their own consciousness are their own monsters. Each look in the mirror shows you a different self. . . . The lost ones return to the same old self and sit there in the corner, laughing or crying.[16]

The rejection of symmetrical form in favor of prose is accompanied by a rejection of the coherent, conscious self; at this stage of the discussion, we cannot glibly call this conjunction coincidental.

We must be careful of jumping to unwarranted conclusions.

16. *The Bourgeois Poet* (New York: Random House, 1964), pp. 95–96.

It is surely not my contention, for example, that all poets writing in America since World War Two fall into the patterns discussed above. But certain generalizations can scarcely be avoided. The overwhelming majority of poets writing in that period implicitly reject the conventional ego as absolute arbiter of experience, and make use of open, organic forms. Of those few preferring symmetrical forms, many of the most significant assert the self's integrity, absurdly, against a background of meaninglessness. What all these poets have in common is an awareness of the impotence of the individual self, the apparent impossibility of reason to organize experience. The majority applaud this abdication; they are happy to emphasize the poem as the expression of the total organism. The minority protest; they are poets of loss. These lines are not absolute. John Berryman, for example, is a poet of loss, and he finds his fragmented self terrifying; Karl Shapiro decries the domination of consciousness and crosses over into prose. But the broad outlines hold up well.

Although there is no place in this study for a detailed examination of the question, it is impossible not to at least raise the obvious corollary to our conclusions. Why is it that postwar poets seem overwhelmingly to favor an escape from the self, while novelists generally prefer the existential position, protesting the loss of the self? There are, of course, exceptions on both sides, like the poets we have noted above, and novelists like Leonard Cohen in *Beautiful Losers.* But our major novelists—Saul Bellow, William Styron, Norman Mailer, Ralph Ellison, John Hawkes in his early work—seem to confirm rather than deny this proposition.

One possible explanation is the fact that the novel, for all of the experimentation of recent decades, is largely dependent on character. And while this is a perfectly reasonable aesthetic judgment, it may be equally valid as a piece of historical analysis. The novel did, after all, begin to come to prominence just after the Renaissance, just after the emergence of the western conception of individual selfhood from the anonymity of the Middle Ages. The novel may be a monument to the conventional ego. If that were the case, then to attempt to create the novel without character could be to risk its destruction; and that risk is quite possibly what the novel has recently experienced.

Poetry, on the other hand, seems to have arisen in most cultures as a product of the collective imagination of those cultures. And when, in lyric poetry, it has become the expression of an individual voice, it has been the voice of the moment, of perception, mood, insight, but not of a sequence of events; lyric poetry has consequently never had the notion of consistent, coherent character at its core.

I am not suggesting, of course, that the genre chosen by a particular writer determines his approach to reality. It would be closer to the other way around, that each genre is equipped to do things that others cannot, and therefore more suitable to given modes of shaping reality. Nor am I proposing an absolute relationship between these factors. Not only is it common for writers to shift from genre to genre (although that would not in itself constitute a serious objection), points of view are complex, and therefore need not be always expressible by a commitment to one extreme or another. However, what I am asserting is that in an age in which there is widespread agreement among writers that the integrity and power of the conventional self is suspect, more novelists have explored the possibilities of reaffirming that self, while more poets have embraced its apparent disintegration.

CHAPTER SIX

The Critical Eye

To this point we have given most of our attention to the writer and his work. We must now turn to the figure without whom the poem could not be said truly to exist, the reader, and his representative (in the sense of both spokesman and guide), the critic. For surely no significant change in the poet's, or the poem's, response to experience could take place without affecting the poem's audience.

We have, in fact, already encountered instances of these changes. The reader of the Objectist poem is involved in the creative process far more thoroughly—or at least far more perceptibly—than previous readers of poetry. In chapter 3, I took advantage of a distinction drawn by Marshall McLuhan. The conventional poem resembles the film, which, sharp in definition, imposes its reality on the relatively passive audience. The Objectist poem, in contrast, like the dots that constitute the television image, which has no definition at all without the perceptual apparatus of the viewer, dramatically implicates the reader in the poem's creation. Frank Kermode, in an interesting essay on T. S. Eliot, uses a term borrowed by Wallace Stevens from Simone Weil, "decreation," as a kind of equivalent to the condition of the electronic dots before the reader transforms them into a coherent image.

> One way to tell them [decreative poets] is by a certain ambiguity in your own response. *The Waste Land,* and also *Hugh Selwyn Mauberley,* can strike you in certain moments as emperors without clothes; discrete poems cobbled into a sequence which is always in-

viting the censure of pretentiousness. It is with your own proper fic-
tive covering that you hide their nakedness and make them wise.
Perhaps there is in *Life Studies* an ambivalence of the same sort.[1]

We—or at least Robert Duncan—might quarrel with the lump-
ing together of Eliot and Pound: ". . . the *Cantos* are central, as
active; and the *Wasteland* or *Four Quartets,* beside the point, as
dramatic."[2] But Kermode's assessment of this kind of poetry,
which certainly includes Pound and Lowell, is accurate, and
clearly raises problems both for the innocent reader and for the
probably less innocent critic. How can we interpret poetry that
includes so significant a variable as the reader's response as part
of its own composition? How can we evaluate a work that so
thoroughly breaks down the barriers between the judge and the
thing to be judged? In fact, this latter difficulty is very much to
the point. How can a criticism which, as we shall see, depends
on being able to isolate the literary work it is considering, deal
with poetry that cannot be so isolated?

In addition, we have already encountered a difficulty inherent
in a fragmentary poem put together the way Pound's *Cantos* is
put together. The conventional poem, we saw in chapter 3, insists that the reader focus in front of the screen, that he perceive the poem as a whole, as well as the component parts that
constitute that whole. The fragmentary poem insists that the
reader focus on the screen, that he experience each fragment in
itself, and find "meaning" in the gaps between fragments rather
than in the fragment's place in a larger vision of things. (Here is
the difference between *The Waste Land* and the *Cantos:* Eliot's
poem allows you to focus in front of the screen, and, as a closed
system, perceive its wholeness; Pound's work, an open system,
defends the absolute integrity of its parts.) But our criticism
prepares us only to apprehend the poem as an isolated, unified

---

1. "A Babylonish Dialect," *T. S. Eliot: The Man and His Work,* ed. Allen Tate
(New York: Dell, 1966), pp. 241–42.
2. Robert Duncan, "Notes on Poetics Regarding Olson's *Maximus,*" *The Poetics
of the New American Poetry,* ed. Donald M. Allen and Warren Tallman (New
York: Grove Press, 1973), p. 189.

entity. If a poem refuses to come to terms with those requirements, how can we interpret or evaluate it?

Before attempting to answer these questions, we must first
arrive at an understanding as to what constitutes "our criticism." In *The Armed Vision,* Stanley Hyman implicitly defined
modern criticism as a series of extraliterary disciplines applied
to literature. While there is certainly something to this definition, it missed a central point. Our literary sensibilities are dominated by one school of criticism whose principles have, until
recently, been so taken for granted as to be beyond discussion,
and which has managed to identify itself as the only "pure"
form of literary criticism available. I am speaking, of course, of
the New Criticism, under whose influence the current generation of scholars and critics have been educated, and whose main
characteristics are precisely those we have found inapplicable to
the new poetry: the isolation of the poem and the embracing of
structural unity in the conventional sense of the term as its in-
dispensable quality.

There is a clear risk of distorting and oversimplifying the New
Critical position, especially since what we are concerned with is
an intellectual atmosphere rather than a specific body of doctrine. As is the case with so many schools of thought, in such
disciplines as psychology and philosophy no less than literary
criticism, those converted to its principles are often less subtle,
less sophisticated in their application, than the school's origina-
tors. Nonetheless, we should be able to reach definitions sufficiently clear for the purposes of our discussion.

In 1941, John Crowe Ransom's *The New Criticism,* which
focused on the work of I. A. Richards, William Empson, T. S.
Eliot, and Yvor Winters, was published. The term, like Modernism, took hold not only as a description of contemporary work,
but as a label that would remain part of literary history. Along
with the critics mentioned above, those literary figures associated with Ransom at Vanderbilt—Robert Penn Warren,
Cleanth Brooks, and Allen Tate—were immediately considered
part of the group. Ultimately, the term would apply to all criticism emphasizing the close reading of text. But at the start, it

was a movement that owed most of its sense of direction to the work done by I. A. Richards, and later his pupil William Empson in the twenties and thirties.

Probably the most important contribution of Richards to the practice of literary criticism was his emphasis on the reader's response to poetry. In *Practical Criticism* (1929), Richards documents, by the use of student responses to unlabeled poetry, his list of interferences that come between the poem and the reader: difficulty in making out its plain sense, differing capacities for sensuous apprehension, differing visual imaginations, mnemonic irrelevances, stock responses, sentimentality, inhibitions, doctrinal adhesions, technical presuppositions, general critical preconceptions.[3]

The chief significance of Richards' approach to literary criticism lies not in the specific nature of the interferences described. Nor does it even lie in the simple fact of examining readers' responses, which, as we shall see, may take very different forms. It is rather that Richards' very notion of interferences implies a pure response to poetry, a response which, although the critic might be willing to admit is difficult or impossible to achieve, becomes the ideal and exclusive goal of the reader. It is not in the least to deny the immense value of being aware of the variables in the individual's response to poetry to point out that Richard's approach leads to the conception of a poem that exists, in theory if nowhere else, in isolation from the reader, whose obligation it then becomes to adapt himself to the objective reality of the poem. Whether or not this is in itself a reasonable proposition is less the issue than whether it can be applied to poetry whose implicit assumptions about the nature of reality define it as a relationship between observer and thing observed. Richards' criticism attempts to separate the observer (the reader) from the thing observed (the poem). And this may very well account for the difficulties New Critical approaches have encountered in dealing with much of the poetry that has been the subject of this book.

3. *Practical Criticism* (New York: Harcourt Brace, 1929), pp. 12–15.

In addition to attempting to isolate legitimate responses to poetry, the experiment upon which *Practical Criticism* was based also removed from consideration all information about the author of the poem. The clear implication was that the poem in itself was not only sufficient to produce a satisfactory effect in the reader, but that the addition of further information might well constitute another interference with the reader's response. As later codified in the well-known essays by W. K. Wimsatt and Monroe C. Beardsley, "The Affective Fallacy" and "The Intentional Fallacy," these two separations of the poem, from the reader on the one hand and the poet on the other, became defining characteristics of the New Criticism.

To be sure, there are significant differences among those who have come to bear the label of this mode of criticism. Ransom's book was in part an attack on the critics he discussed. And, in an essay like "Pure and Impure Poetry," Robert Penn Warren could indeed protest against the notion that a poem could be totally separated from its human context. Nonetheless, Warren does not repudiate warnings against the dangers of interference. And when all is said and done, there can be no denying that twentieth-century criticism, as represented by the figures we have been discussing, has succeeded in placing an emphasis on the text itself, as opposed to any extraneous phenomena, the like of which has probably never been seen before.

This concentration on the poem in itself had the logical consequence of requiring structural principles that could be located in the poem without reference to any external factors, and which soon became indispensible for purposes of both interpretation and evaluation. Of the many examples of this approach it is perhaps appropriate to cite its expression by the namer of this criticism, John Crowe Ransom, in his essay "The Concrete Universal: Observations on the Understanding of Poetry." Toward the end of his piece, Ransom says: "Kant's understanding therefore chooses to regard poetry as a single and powerful though complicated action; and that is the kind of view which is deeply coveted by the modern critics. It is a complete view—except for one reservation. . . ." The one reservation is that Kant dealt with short poetical passages or poems; what of the longer work? Even there, Ransom sees in the moral Universal, his unity-granting principle, a source of structure that will hold the poem together. "It cannot often be that the action focuses upon a single metaphorical or metaphysical moment. The chances are, overwhelmingly, that the moral Universal in such cases is a considerable and organized sequence of intellectual ideas, or of historical events, embodied for action and working themselves out. . . ."[4]

In these last remarks, we can easily recognize the critical dicta by whose authority critics like Noel Stock reduce works like the *Cantos* to a series of fragments. And if we return to the anecdote of the African natives watching the film recounted in chapter 3, we will understand from a new perspective the connection between the isolation of the poem and the emphasis on unity of structure. The natives, who could not focus in front of the screen but on it, also could not isolate the action of the film from the reality surrounding it and therefore wanted to know what had happened to actors who had moved out of the picture. Separating the poem from other realities and discovering its unified structure are related concepts. We shall later consider the possibility that if the isolation is removed our notion of structure must be modified.

The concern with unity of vision in turn leads to a renewed involvement in the intellectual aspects of poetry. Or rather, since the importance of the content of a poem had never been seriously questioned before our own time, a new involvement with the microscopic examination of the intellectual aspects of poetry. For if our primary purpose is to relate the "message" of the poem to commonly recognizable experience, our attention will be on that relation. But if we isolate the poem from experience, then our intellectual curiosity must force the poem to turn in on itself. It is only reasonable, then, that I. A. Richards' work would lead directly to William Empson's.

In *Seven Types of Ambiguity* (1930), Empson identifies as the

4. *Poems and Essays* (New York: Vintage, 1955), pp. 184–85.

essence of poetry the resonance of its language, which operates in several ways at once, and proposes "to consider a series of definite and detachable ambiguities, in which several large and crude meanings can be separated out, and to arrange them in order of increasing distance from simple statement and logical expression." Irritated by unexplained beauty,[5] the critic embarks on a series of brilliant readings which certainly enrich our understandings of the poems, though maybe not their beauty. Aware that there are significant dimensions of the poem he is not investigating, Empson nonetheless concentrates his attention, and perhaps helps concentrate the attention of many critics after him, on the rationally apprehensible aspects of the work.

One of the finest consequences of this mode of literary criticism is Cleanth Brooks's *The Well Wrought Urn* (1947). But the stance Brooks adopts in that book also illustrates the bias toward the rational in so much modern criticism. "Few of us are prepared to accept the statement that the language of poetry is the language of paradox. . . . Yet there is a sense in which paradox is the language appropriate and inevitable to poetry."[6] To be sure, Brooks uses the term in its broadest possible sense and does not consider it to be intellectual rather than emotional, or rational rather than irrational—in theory. But in fact the emphasis of the critical pieces falls necessarily on various types of irony, which must surely partake of the rational, and which is quite dependent upon establishing a fixed point of view from which the irony can be perceived. And if there is any conspicuous difference between the poetry of Eliot and Modernism on the one hand, and that of the postwar period on the other, it is the considerable muting of irony in the latter—with such rule-proving exceptions as Randall Jarrell, Karl Shapiro, and Delmore Schwartz.

As we have already conceded, it is not really possible to talk of the New Criticism as if it were a precisely ordered discipline,

5. New York: Meridian, 1955, pp. 10, 13.
6. New York: Harcourt, Brace and World, 1947, p. 3.

complete with an unambiguous membership list. Nonetheless, it is possible to observe that there are certain dominating tendencies in modern criticism which have collectively, if somewhat vaguely, been labeled the New Criticism, and that these tendencies pretty regularly include the isolation of the poem, the emphasis on its coherent structure, and the detailed examination of intellectual components of that structure. It is also reasonable to assert that these tendencies are closely related, that whether the poem's isolation leads to concern with that which is consciously apprehensible, or whether the reliance on consciousness isolates the poem, the connection is there, and consequently justifies our identification of a complex of critical attitudes as a significant force in modern literature.

The fact is, however, that this mode of criticism reveals itself to be totally unsuitable in dealing with poetry that has abandoned the "ego-position"; for, to make use of Charles Olson's term for conventional poetic perspective, the New Criticsm is itself bound to the "ego-position." The obvious question, then, is why have we developed a critical approach so unsuitable to the poetry of its time? And the answer is that it is not at all unsuitable, and that, in fact, it is the poetry we have been discussing that was not, and could not have been, considered suitable until after the Second World War. Before then, Williams was not in academic favor, while Pound was known for poems like "Mauberley"—which, while its fragmentation and use of personae look forward to the *Cantos,* is one of its author's few ironic works, and therefore at least partially accessible to the New Criticism—or simply held in incomprehensible awe; the other poets of the new self come later.

So that the New Criticism, inappropriate as it is to the poetry we have been discussing, especially Objectist poetry, has clear usefulness. Another glance at the definitions we have established for it, with the object of deducing the area of its most fruitful application, should uncover at once the correct fit: Metaphysical poetry, or the poetry of the Neo-Metaphysical revival. Here is a poetry dominated by the intellectually intricate conceit, by wit and irony, a poetry whose internal structure is strong enough to permit the poem to be studied in isolation more successfully than any other poetic mode. And this insight makes us recall that T. S. Eliot's famous review of Sir Herbert Grierson's collection of Metaphysical verse, "The Metaphysical Poets" (1921), did, in fact, initiate a period both of renewed interest in the Metaphysicals and of sophisticated imitation of their work. Poets like W. H. Auden, Léonie Adams, Louise Bogan, Elinor Wylie, and Stanley Kunitz, were all caught up, at least temporarily, by the possibilities of Metaphysical verse; even such unlikely figures as Theodore Roethke and Robert Lowell began their careers most obviously under this pervasive influence.

We may pause to notice briefly the implications this association of the New Criticism and the Metaphysical revival has for the nature of criticism. It suggests that schools of criticism are devised to account for particular modes of poetic expression, and therefore do not necessarily have the intrinsic validity they all claim. The fact is, we have not enough experience of the practice of criticism—it was really not a large scale, self-conscious phenomenon until the twentieth century—to be able to prove or disprove that hypothesis. There is at the least enough uncertainty to justify the suspicions we have expressed at the application of the New Criticism to so much poetry that does not seem to make the slightest attempt to meet its standards.

We may also observe that among the possible reasons for the emergence of literary criticism as a significant discipline, one of the most important may well be the confusion as to the legitimate perspective a poem, or indeed, any work of literature should utilize. Until now, the perspective has been taken for granted. It has been the commonly shared cultural point of view. But our own age might well be named the "age of choice." We have available to us a multiplicity of perspectives, of definitions of the self. And since there is no possibility of coming to terms with the poem without understanding its implicit version of the self, and of the self's relation to the rest of reality, commentaries are necessary to elucidate, directly or indirectly, the perspective of the poem.

Once the inevitability of the New Criticism has been called into question, many of its assertions become difficult to defend. The idea that other modes of criticism in frequent use are "impure" in their application of extraliterary disciplines to the study of literature, while the New Criticism is the only approach devoted to the poem itself is totally dependent upon the assumption that it is possible to isolate the poem from the rest of experience, from the poet's as well as from the reader's. What before seemed an attempt to exclude the extraneous now appears to be an attempt to separate the poem from the true basis of its existence. And the New Criticism's attacks on, say, the political criticism of the Marxists, now seems rather disingenuous in its total denial of political reality, and makes us wonder whether or not the exclusion of contemporary events from discussions of the poem is not in itself a defense of the status quo, and whether the New Critical definition of structure is not based on the same assumptions that defend western political institutions against their critics. And the fact that the group of critics who adopted the New Criticism and gave it its name, John Crowe Ransom and his colleagues at Vanderbilt, are by and large to be found among the politically conservative southern agrarians who appear in *I'll Take My Stand: The South and the Agrarian Tradition* (1930), suggests, without ascribing conspiratorial motives or conscious designs of any sort to these writers, that there may be as much of an affinity between strictly formalist criticism and conservative politics on the one hand, as there more evidently is between socially oriented criticism and political activism on the other. That is to say, the connection is not always there, but it very often is.

Our position then must be that the critic is in some respects like the grammarian, who, while he operates as a stabilizing influence on language, is ultimately responsive to significant, broad-based changes in the way language is used. The critic must surely comment on the degree to which a poem has succeeded in accomplishing what it set out to do. But he probably should not determine what the poem should be, or how it should be it. In fact, in an age like our own, in which there is less controversy about the distinction between good and bad poetry than there is about the distinction between poetry and non-poetry, it is probably the critic's chief task to describe what the aims and standards of the given poem are, and only secondarily to evaluate its success. It has, of course, been long taken for granted that the critic would not attempt to impose his own assumptions upon the poem. The point of our discussion is that included among these assumptions must be the ego's prerogative of ordering and interpreting experience, and the consequent structural characteristics with which the poem is endowed. This structure is no more natural than the ability to focus in front of the screen was to the African natives in the anecdote cited by Marshall McLuhan. It is a single legitimate method of putting together a poem, and critical principles derived from the same view of man's relation to experience are perfectly legitimate when applied to it. However, ego-based poetry and the New Criticism are very much like Newtonian physics encountering the Einsteinian universe. They are special cases, which, within certain limits, work perfectly, but which cannot make claim, any more than Einsteinian physics, to being absolute truth. And this analogy, I hope, is not mere show. For Newtonian physics, with its vision of a closed system and its faith in the ability of rational constructs to describe phenomena, is indeed ego based, while Einsteinian physics (using the term to refer to twentieth-century physics in general), centered on the relativity of time and space and the principle of indeterminacy, abandons totally the ego's world of common-sense reality.

The problems created by the application of the New Criticism to the newer poetry may be divided into two classes. First, there are the obvious instances, for example, Noel Stock's critique of the *Cantos,* which we discussed in Chapter Three. Here, the result is to reject the work that does not measure up to standards, or at least to apologize for it. This is, in a sense, the less harmful, since when the reader's intuition that he has encountered remarkable poetry contradicts his definition of the poem, he is in many cases willing to re-examine his preconceptions. And although the work of an Ezra Pound disobeys so many of the rules, it has not, in fact, been easy to dispose of, and if it is rejected finally as one of the major works of its time, it will be because of a diminished estimate of the poet's ear or his eye rather than because of any formulae. The second category is more difficult to point out and to defend against. It includes responses to such works as Robert Lowell's *Life Studies,* which may be interpreted with perfectly satisfactory results with the help of the New Criticism, especially since it is written by a poet who came to maturity under that critical approach and who began his career distinctly under its influence. However, we may argue nonetheless that there is a dimension to the poetry that is not given appropriate attention unless a more comprehensive vision of the self is accepted, and that it is paradoxically true that unless that self be understood to encompass all that it perceives, the individual as individual can be only imperfectly represented.

With these warnings in mind, however, and with the awareness that those of us educated while the New Criticism was a dominant force—which includes the great majority of critics practicing today—are subject to biases frequently too subtle easily to be perceived, there is not much point in making a whipping boy of a methodology which is itself a symptom rather than a cause of the conventional notion of the self. For it is still true that the self's inability to govern is an occasion for dismay rather than joy for all but a distinct minority, and is experienced as a loss, not an escape. It is in any case more likely that criticism will trail poetry rather than the other way around, and we might expect that by now a criticism—or criticisms—not dominated by the self in isolation, and therefore not postulating the poem in isolation, would be beginning to emerge, not necessarily as a direct response to the poetry we have been discussing, but as a reaction to the world of ideas and sensibilities that produced that poetry. And the fact is that there are evidences of such critical methodologies, some of them rising from the still warm ashes of the New Criticism itself.

Since the New Criticism has been found lacking by us chiefly in its isolation of the poem, it is appropriate to divide the newer criticisms into those that return our attention to the poet's creative act, and those that involve us once more in the reader's responses. And we should make it clear from the start that we will not be talking about simple regression to older modes. For among few readers of poetry today has the notion of the primacy of the text been lost.

Walter Ong, for example, one of those who has refocused attention on the writing of the poem, does not concern himself with the writer's intention but with the modality of his expression. Ong has studied the differences between oral and written poetry, and in this endeavor he cannot be called one of McLuhan's followers, since Ong himself was one of the early pioneers in this area, and is, in fact, cited as one of McLuhan's sources in *The Gutenberg Galaxy*. In one of Ong's first influential essays, he implicitly identifies the New Criticism with poetry as it appears on the written page, and reminds us that the poem is essentially an oral construct.

> Many of the critics just cited [Cleanth Brooks, W. K. Wimsatt, I. A. Richards, René Wellek, Austin Warren, and T. S. Eliot] as preoccupied with objects, structures, skeletons, and stratified systems have pressed the point that poetry belongs to the world of sound even while dissolving this world in explanation based on spatial analogies. But to consider the work of literature in its primary oral and aural existence, we must enter more profoundly into this world of sound as such, the I-Thou world where, through the mysterious interior resonance which sound best of all provides, persons commune with persons, reaching one another's interiors in a way in which one can never reach the interior of an "object." Here, instead of reducing words to objects, urns, or even icons, we take them as what they are even more basically, as utterances, that is to say, cries. All verbalization, including all literature, is radically a cry, a sound emitted from the interior of a person, a modification of one's exhalation of breath which retains the intimate connection with life which we find in breath itself, and which registers in the etymology of the word spirit, that is, breath.[7]

7. "A Dialect of Aural and Objective Correlatives," *Approaches to the Poem: Modern Essays in the Analysis and Interpretation of Poetry*, ed. John Oliver Perry (San Francisco: Chandler, 1965), p. 244. The essay originally appeared in *Essays in Criticism*, 8 (January 1958).

Ong goes on to say that although the "cry" is an assertion of the interior self, that self then goes on to lose its "interiority" by dragging in and involving other selves to share that interior existence. This, in fact, sounds very much like Charles Olson's Projective act, and Ong's emphasis on the centrality of breath encourages that comparison. In any case, it is clear that this theory of poetry is far more appropriate to the work we have been studying than those theories that have for so long monopolized our critical sensibilities. And if we cannot pretend to have found the "absolute criticism," the critical approach that would remain consistently valid no matter the nature of the poetry to which it was applied, we can at least endorse a criticism whose assumptions about the self's place in the scheme of things are compatible with the work it criticizes.

But Ong's remarks cited above belong most properly to the ontology of poetry. For practical criticism, we must turn again to the man who is most responsible for initiating the reign of the New Criticism, I. A. Richards. If we look back on Richards' work from our own perspective, we may well come to feel that its major contribution was its emphasis on the act of reading the poem. Now it is true that Richards was interested in examining the reader's response in order to eliminate the unjustified inclusion of certain extraliterary variables in that response, with the result that the text, especially in the hands of some of Richards' followers, became completely isolated, an object in and of itself. But the most enduring insight of *Practical Criticism* is not that the reader's response is illegitimate, but rather that he must be educated in the process of experiencing the poem. And so we are directed again to the study of responses to the work of literature.

David Bleich, Walter Slatoff, and Stanley Fish are among the more prominent of those critics who have, in fact, turned in that direction.[8] Stanley Fish is most appropriate to our discussion precisely because he is very much aware of the relationship of

8. See David Bleich, *Readings and Feelings* (Urbana, Ill.: National Council of Teachers of English, 1975) and Walter J. Slatoff, *With Respect to Readers: Dimensions of Literary Response* (Ithaca, N.Y.: Cornell University Press, 1970).

his work to Richards'. In the appendix to *Self-Consuming Artifacts*, "Literature in the Reader: Affective Stylists," Fish directly confronts the Affective Fallacy, the idea that the reader's responses must be separated from the meaning of the poem. Fish demonstrates that the proper question to ask of literature is not what it means, or even how it means, but rather what it does. The poem's existence as a work of art is really located at the intersection between poem and reader—the mirror image, incidentally, of Pound's locating the Imagist poem at the intersection between outer world and poet—and it is that intersection that commands our interest. Most striking for our purposes, however, is Fish's attack on the notion that the poem can be considered "objectively":

> A criticism that regards "the poem itself as an object of specifically critical judgment" extends this forgetting that the poem is experienced in time into a principle; it transforms a temporal experience into a spatial one; it steps back and in a single glance takes in a whole (sentence, page, work) which the reader knows (if at all) only bit by bit, moment by moment. It is a criticism that takes as its (self-restricted) area the physical dimensions of the artifact and within these dimensions it marks out beginnings, middles, and ends, discovers frequency distributions, traces out patterns of imagery, diagrams strata of complexity (vertical of course), all without ever taking into account the relationship (if any) between its data and their affective force. Its question is what goes into the work rather than what the work goes into. It is "objective" in exactly the wrong way, because it determinedly ignores what is objectively true about the *activity* of reading. Analysis in terms of doings and happenings is on the other hand truly objective because it recognizes the fluidity, "the movingness," of the meaning experience and because it directs us to where the action is—the active and activating consciousness of the reader.[9]

To return again to the metaphor based on preliterate natives viewing a film, which we found so useful in approaching the *Cantos*, Fish's attack is leveled directly against the practice of focusing in front of the screen; in exhorting us to be aware of

9. Berkeley: University of California Press, 1972, p. 401. Originally printed in *New Literary History*, 2 (Autumn, 1970).

the temporality of the poem, that is, to experience it piece by piece, he is telling us to focus on the screen. By an entirely different route, and by use of distinct frames of reference, we have come round to almost identical notions of how to come to terms with the poem. And by insisting that the poem in a sense exists in the reader—again like a McLuhan-based metaphor, the television picture which is focused in the viewer's eye—Fish points out the mechanism by which the expanded self of a poem like *Life Studies* can be perceived (for the reader has become, at least for the time, a version of that self). Fish ably defends his perspective; but we might add to that defense the fact that his mode of criticism is infinitely more useful, not simply in dealing with the *Cantos* and *Life Studies,* but with the work of Williams and Olson, Lowell's *Notebooks,* Berryman's *Dream Songs,* and even some of Plath's work, to restrict ourselves to poetry we have considered, than the criticism he rejects.

It should come as no surprise to us to discover that these two modes of criticism—one concentrating on the process of creation and the other on the reader's response—should be intimately related. And they do, in fact, come together in the work of Walter Ong. Continuing his investigations of the differences between oral and written verbalization, Ong explores the greater necessity of the literate author to create a fictional audience to replace the perceived reactions of the oral author. In the end, just as the writer must put on masks, so must the reader put on his own mask in order to relate to the work of literature. And although these masks exist in all human communication, including oral, and even personal oral communication, there is an existential dimension in direct human contact that helps remove at least some of those masks.

> No matter what pitch of frankness, directness, or authenticity he may strive for, the writer's mask and the reader's are less removable than those of the oral communicator and his hearer. For writing is itself an indirection. . . . This makes writing not less but more interesting, although perhaps less noble than speech. . . . Present-day confessional writings . . . likes to make an issue of stripping off all masks. Observant literary critics and psychiatrists, however, do

not need to be told that confessional literature is likely to wear the most masks of all.[10]

Just as Stanley Fish attacks the Affective Fallacy, so Walter Ong, without mentioning it by name, goes after the Intentional Fallacy. Not that Ong suggests we ought to take into account the author's understandir.g of the "meaning" of his work. But we must take into account the masks intended for the use of his audience. In other words, Ong's criticism takes us another step away from the isolation of the poem as a discrete entity that may be studied in and of itself. And, as we can see in the remarks cited above that parallel our own responses to Confessional poetry, it is a form of criticism far more suited to poetry that has "escaped the self" than more familiar critical approaches.

Our attempt to define the escape from the self is now complete. We have seen in the attention accorded to Norman Brown and Marshall McLuhan evidence that this escape has attracted our cultural imagination. We have examined the expression of that imagination in recent American poetry. And finally, we have discovered emerging trends in modern criticism, which take into account—although they display no special awareness of the particular writers we have been considering—the requirements of this new view of the self and its relation to the rest of reality. There remains only to speculate on the place of this conception of the self in literary history. And that will be the subject of a brief final chapter.

10. "The Writer's Audience Is Always a Fiction," *PMLA*, 90 (January 1975), 20–21.

CHAPTER SEVEN

A Retrospect

IT is beyond the scope of this book to determine whether the phenomenon under consideration—the escape from the self in contemporary poetry—is unique throughout the world. We may be content to remark that the strength of British poetry in the twentieth century has been more traditional than American poetry. Yeats, far more committed to conventional form than major American poets, stands alone. And even a poet so under the influence of surrealism—and therefore a challenger of the traditional self—as Dylan Thomas prefers regularity of stanzaic pattern and meter. D. H. Lawrence, as is so often the case, is an exception, and in that sense is an unwritten chapter of this book. But postwar British poetry has been largely composed of off-shoots of American sources of energy, most obviously Projectivism and Confessional verse. It may be more than coincidence that this reversal of historic roles occurs at precisely the moment that the escape from the self is a representative component of our cultural consciousness. It is certainly possible that America's relatively less rigid commitment to a specific version of the self has contributed to this shift in momentum.

A more legitimate object of our attention is the question of how lasting a vision of reality we have been dealing with, of how important a place it will hold in the history of American poetry. It first seemed as if the dominant use of perspectives other than the conscious self began with Pound, was developed by the Objectist poets, and became the rule rather than the exception after the Second World War. This may well be the case. If so, we might expect a long period during which free verse would remain the nearly exclusively used rhythmic form, in which alogical principles of organization would prevail, in which coldly detached perception and deep sprung sources of imagery would continue to replace the ego's mediation.

However, what evidence there is suggests that so thorough and longlasting a triumph of the new self is not likely. Already Marshall McLuhan and Norman Brown, never totally respectable in orthodox circles, have ceased to command even terribly much abuse. The sixties, with their attempt to green America, made the new self part of not simply popular, but mass, culture. But the sixties, which in some far-fetched way could be traced from Pound to Williams to Ginsberg and the Beat Generation to the Hippies, have passed.

In 1975, the National Book Award was won by Marilyn Hacker for a book that contained no fewer than seven sestinas, twelve sonnets, and a villanelle.[1] Projectivist verse would still probably win a head count among young poets in the United States today, but to this point, the generation that produced Robert Creeley and Joel Oppenheimer has not been succeeded by poets of their worth. And if M. L. Rosenthal was premature in suggesting that the end of Confessional poetry coincided with the deaths of Sylvia Plath and Theodore Roethke in 1963, it seems nonetheless true that that poetic mode, in its purest forms, did not long outlast them.[2]

But most significant of all, it seems to me, is the change effected by Robert Lowell in his *Notebook* poems, discussed in chapter 4 above, in which he rearranged in chronological order the poems of *History,* and removed as inappropriate the more personal poems of *Lizzie and Harriet.* It is not simply that Lowell is one of our most important postwar writers that suggests we take seriously the directions in which he moves, but also the fact that Lowell—from the Neo-Metaphysical verse of *Lord*

1. *Presentation Piece* (New York: Viking, 1974).
2. *The New Poets* (New York: Oxford University Press, 1967), pp. 112–13.

Weary's Castle through the self-expanding perspectives of *Life Studies* and *Notebook 1967–68*—has been very much in tune with prevailing cultural sensibilities. It is quite likely that his imposition of temporal order and the separation of public and private represent a more widespread rejection of the search—in its extremest form—for the alternative to the ego-position.

But rejection of the extreme is not necessarily total repudiation. Although Norman Brown never did succeed in making clear to us what his new consciousness would be like, or what manner of civilization could embody it, he did powerfully reinforce our sense that our methods of organizing responses to experience were neither natural nor inevitable. And if Marshall McLuhan never made us feel quite at home in the Global Village, he did provide concrete instances of ways in which our perceptions of reality alter that reality. Similarly, the poetry we have been examining has left a permanent mark on the poet's means of organizing the poem. Free verse has made so profound an impression that even the minority that use conventional meter use it with a freedom that would have been impossible before this century. Juxtaposition in its purest forms may be rarely employed these days, but some modifications, with the edges less jagged, are as common as montage in the cinema. And for all of Marilyn Hacker's sestinas, the real showpiece of her book, "The Navigators," would have been inconceivable before the Confessional breakthroughs of Lowell, Anne Sexton, and the rest.

Most important, however, is the sensibility behind the traits that embody it. We have become aware of what was, as Stanley Burnshaw correctly points out, always implicit in poetry: that it is an expression not only of consciousness but of the entire human organism. In an age in which from most philosophical and scientific perspectives conventional logic is simply a strait jacket, it is hardly surprising that the emphasis should fall on other than rational expressions of selfhood. Nor is it surprising that in the development of a methodology that could communicate more of the arational than ever attempted by our literature, there would be a rush to extremes that would not only balance the contributions of consciousness but also threaten to overwhelm them. But in the process of pulling back from extremes, what is most striking is just how large a proportion of the new techniques is now taken for granted, just how much of an at least partial escape from the self has become a fundamental condition of poetry.

Index